The Adventures of
TOM SAWYER

by
Mark Twain

Original Novel abridged for
Modern Readers

LITTLE SCHOLARZ PVT LTD.
INDIA

This edition first originated and published in 2019

LITTLE SCHOLARZ Pvt Ltd.

12-H, New Daryaganj Road, Opp. Officers' Mess, New Delhi-110002 (India)
Phone # 91-11-23275124, 23275224, 23245124, 23261567
email : info@littlescholarz.com
website : www.littlescholarz.com
for online purchase : www.rameshpublishinghouse.com

© LITTLE SCHOLARZ Pvt. Ltd.

THE ADVENTURES OF TOM SAWYER

ISBN: 978-93-86063-28-1

HSN Code: 49011010

Book Code: S-418

No part of this book may be reproduced or utilized in any form or by any means, electronic or mechanical including photocopying, recording or by any information storage and retrieval system, without permission in writing from the publisher.

Contents

- Chapter-1 ... 5
- Chapter-2 ... 9
- Chapter-3 ... 16
- Chapter-4 ... 20
- Chapter-5 ... 25
- Chapter-6 ... 30
- Chapter-7 ... 37
- Chapter-8 ... 41
- Chapter-9 ... 45
- Chapter-10 ... 51
- Chapter-11 ... 55
- Chapter-12 ... 58
- Chapter-13 ... 62
- Chapter-14 ... 70
- Chapter-15 ... 74
- Chapter-16 ... 78
- Chapter-17 ... 86
- Chapter-18 ... 89
- Chapter-19 ... 94
- Chapter-20 ... 96
- Chapter-21 ... 100
- Chapter-22 ... 104
- Chapter-23 ... 107
- Chapter-24 ... 112

- Chapter-25 ... 113
- Chapter-26 ... 117
- Chapter-27 ... 123
- Chapter-28 ... 125
- Chapter-29 ... 129
- Chapter-30 ... 135
- Chapter-31 ... 140
- Chapter-32 ... 143
- Chapter-33 ... 145
- Chapter-34 ... 151
- Chapter-35 ... 153

- Conclusion ... 157
- Glossary (word-meanings) ... 158
- Short & Long Questions ... 159

❑❑❑

Chapter 1

Aunt Polly had been looking anxiously for Tom since long. She called him a number of times, but got no response. Then she shouted loudly.

There was a slight noise behind her and she turned just in time to seize a small boy by the slack of his roundabout and arrest his flight.

"There! I might 'a' thought of that closet. What you been doing in there?"

Tom was rolling jam in his mouth. When he smelt danger from aunt, he said,

"My! Look behind you, aunt!"

The old lady whirled round, and the lad fled on the instant, scrambled up the high board-fence, and disappeared over it.

His aunt Polly stood surprised a moment, and then broke into a gentle laugh.

"What you been doing in there?" asked Aunt Polly.

"Spare the rod and spile the child, as the Good Book says. But he's my own dead sister's boy, poor thing, and I ain't got the heart to lash him, somehow. He'll play hookey this afternoon I'll just be obleeged to make him work, to-morrow, to punish him," said she to herself.

Tom did play hookey, and he had a very good time. He got back home barely in season to help Jim, the small colored boy, when he had done three-fourths of the work. Tom's younger brother (or rather half-brother) Sid was already through with his part of the work (picking up chips), for he was a quiet boy, and had no adventurous, troublesome ways.

While Tom was eating his supper, Aunt Polly asked him some clever questions. Actually, she wanted to trap him into damaging revealments. She wanted to know if he had gone a swimming. But Tom saw through it and said, "Some of us pumped on our heads—mine's damp yet. See?"

Aunt Polly was vexed, and the trouble vanished out of Tom's face.

Within two minutes, or even less, he had forgotten all his troubles, because a new and powerful interest bore them down and drove them out of his mind for the time. This new interest was a valued novelty in whistling, which he had just acquired from a negro, and he was suffering to practise it undisturbed. Diligence and attention soon gave him the knack of it, and he strode down the street with his mouth full of harmony and his soul full of gratitude.

The summer evenings were long. It was not dark, yet. Presently Tom checked his whistle. A stranger was before him—a boy a shade larger than himself. This boy was well dressed, too—well dressed on a week-day. Neither boy spoke. They kept face to face and eye to eye all the time.

Both the boys seemed to be in a fighting mood, but neither took an initiative, and a war of words between the two continued for some pretty long minutes.

In an instant both boys were rolling and tumbling in the dirt. Presently through the fog of battle Tom appeared, seated astride the new boy, and pounding him with his fists. "Holler 'nuff!" said he.

At last the stranger got out a smothered "'Nuff!" and Tom let him up.

The new boy went off brushing the dust from his clothes, sobbing and snuffling.

He got home pretty late that night, and climbed cautiously in at the window. When aunt saw the state his clothes were in her resolution to turn his Saturday holiday into captivity at hard labor became adamantine in its firmness.

Chapter 2

Saturday morning was come, and all the summer world was bright and fresh, and brimming with life.

Tom appeared on the sidewalk with a bucket of whitewash and a long-handled brush. He surveyed the fence, and all gladness left him and a deep melancholy settled down upon his spirit.

Thirty yards of board fence nine feet high. Sighing, he dipped his brush and passed it along the topmost plank; repeated the operation; did it again and sat down on a tree-box discouraged.

Jim came skipping out at the gate with a tin pail, and singing Buffalo Gals. Bringing water from the town pump had always been hateful work in Tom's eyes, before, but now it did not strike him so.

"Say, Jim, I'll fetch the water if you'll whitewash some," said Tom.

He remembered that there was company at the pump. White, mulatto, and negro boys and girls were always there waiting their turns, resting, trading playthings, quarrelling, fighting, skylarking. Tom said:

"Say, Jim, I'll fetch the water if you'll whitewash some."

Jim shook his head and said "Old Missis had told me to go an' git dis water an' not stop foolin' roun' wid anybody. She 'lowed SHE'D 'tend to de whitewashin'."

"Oh, never you mind what she said, Jim. That's the way she always talks. Gimme the bucket. SHE won't ever know. I'll give you a marvel. I'll give you a white alley!"

Jim began to waver.

"And besides, if you will I'll show you my sore toe."

Jim was only human—this attraction was too much for him. He put down his pail, took the white alley, and bent over the toe with absorbing interest while the bandage was being unwound. In another moment he was flying down the street with his pail and a tingling rear, Tom was whitewashing with vigor, and Aunt Polly was retiring from the field with a slipper in her hand and triumph in her eye.

But Tom's energy did not last. He began to think of the fun he had planned for this day. He got out his worldly wealth and examined it—bits of toys, marbles, and trash; enough to buy an exchange of WORK, maybe, but not half enough to buy so much as half an hour of pure freedom. At this dark and hopeless moment an inspiration burst upon him!

He took up his brush and went tranquilly to work. Ben Rogers hove in sight presently. Ben's gait was the hop-skip-and-jump. He was eating an apple, and giving a long, melodious whoop, at intervals. He was personating a steamboat. He was boat and captain and engine-bells combined, so he had to imagine himself standing on his own hurricane-deck giving the orders and executing them.

"Stop her, sir! Ting-a-ling-ling!" The headway ran almost out, and he drew up slowly toward the sidewalk.

"Set her back on the stabboard! Ting-a-ling-ling! Chow! ch-chow-wow! Chow!" His right hand, meantime, describing stately circles—for it was representing a forty-foot wheel.

Tom went on whitewashing—paid no attention to the steamboat. Ben stared a moment and then said: "Hi-YI! YOU'RE up a stump, ain't you!"

No answer. Tom surveyed his last touch with the eye of an artist, then he gave his brush another gentle sweep and surveyed the result, as before. Ben ranged up alongside of him. Tom's mouth watered for the apple, but he stuck to his work. Ben said:

"Hello, old chap, you got to work, hey?"

"Say—I'm going in a-swimming, I am. Don't you wish you could? But of course you'd druther WORK—wouldn't you?"

Tom contemplated the boy a bit, and said:

"What do you call work? Does a boy get a chance to whitewash a fence every day?"

Ben stopped nibbling his apple. Tom swept his brush daintily back and forth—Ben watching every move and getting more and more interested. Presently he said:

"Say, Tom, let ME whitewash a little."

"No—no—Ben. You see, Aunt Polly's awful particular about this fence—I reckon there ain't one boy in a thousand, maybe two thousand, that can do it the way it's got to be done."

"No—is that so? Oh come, now—lemme just try. Tom."

"Ben, I'd like to, honest injun; but Aunt Polly—well, Jim wanted to do it, but she wouldn't let him; Sid wanted to do it, and she wouldn't let Sid. Now don't you see how I'm fixed? If you was to tackle this fence and anything was to happen to it—"

"Oh, shucks, I'll be just as careful. Now lemme try. Say—I'll give you the core of my apple."

"Well, here—No, Ben, now don't. I'm afeard—"

"I'll give you ALL of it!"

Tom gave up the brush with reluctance in his face, but alacrity in his heart. And while the late steamer Big Missouri worked and sweated in the sun, the retired artist sat on a barrel in the shade close by, dangled his legs, munched his apple, and planned the slaughter of more innocents.

By the time Ben was fagged out, Tom had traded the next chance to Billy Fisher for a kite, in good repair; and when he played out, Johnny Miller bought in for a dead rat and a string to swing it with—and so on.

Now, Tom was literally rolling in wealth. He had besides the things before mentioned, twelve marbles, part of a jews-harp, a piece of blue bottle-glass to look through, a spool cannon, a key that wouldn't unlock anything, a fragment of chalk, a glass stopper of a decanter, a tin soldier, a couple of tadpoles, six fire-crackers, a kitten with only one eye, a brass doorknob, a dog-collar—but no dog—the handle of a knife, four pieces of orange-peel, and a dilapidated old window sash.

He had had a nice, good, idle time all the while—plenty of company —and the fence had three coats of whitewash on it!

Tom had discovered a great law of human action, without knowing it—namely, that in order to make a man or a boy covet a thing, it is only necessary to make the thing difficult to attain. If he had been a great and wise philosopher, he would now have comprehended that Work consists of whatever a body is OBLIGED to do, and that Play consists of whatever a body is not obliged to do.

Chapter 3

Tom presented himself before Aunt Polly. "Mayn't I go and play now, aunt? It's all done."

Aunt Polly placed small trust in such evidence. She went out to see for herself. When she found the entire fence whitewashed, and not only whitewashed but elaborately coated and recoated, and even a streak added to the ground, her astonishment was almost unspeakable. Then he skipped out.

Tom hastened toward the public square of the village, where two "military" companies of boys had met for conflict, according to previous appointment. Tom was General of one of these armies, Joe Harper (a bosom friend) General of the other. These two great commanders did not fight in person—but sat together and conducted the field operations

He saw a lovely little blue-eyed girl in the garden.

by orders delivered through aides-de-camp. Tom's army won a great victory, after a long and hard-fought battle.

As Tom was passing by the house where Jeff Thatcher lived, he saw a new lovely little blue-eyed girl in the garden. A certain Amy Lawrence vanished out of his heart and left not even a memory of herself behind.

Tom began to "show off" in all sorts of absurd boyish ways, in order to win her admiration. Then he saw that the little girl was wending her way toward the house. She tossed a pansy over the fence a moment before she disappeared.

He picked it and hopped away with the treasure and disappeared round the corner.

He buttoned the flower inside his jacket, next his heart—or next his stomach, possibly, for he was not much posted in anatomy.

He returned, now, and hung about the fence till nightfall, "showing off," as before; but the girl never exhibited herself again. Finally he strode home reluctantly, with his poor head full of visions.

All through supper his spirits were so high that his aunt wondered "what had got into the child."

He wandered far from the accustomed haunts of boys, and sought desolate places that were in harmony with his spirit. Then he thought of his flower. He got it out, rumpled and wilted. He wondered if she would pity him if she knew? Or would she turn coldly away like all the hollow world? At last he rose up sighing and departed in the darkness.

About half-past nine or ten o'clock he came along the deserted street to where the Adored Unknown lived. He climbed the fence, threaded his stealthy way through the plants, till he stood under that window; then he laid him down on the ground under it, disposing himself upon his back, with his hands clasped upon his breast and holding his poor wilted flower.

And thus he would die—out in the cold world, with no shelter over his homeless head. And thus SHE would see him when she looked out upon the glad morning, and oh! would she drop one little tear upon his poor, lifeless form.

Suddenly, the window went up, a maid-servant's discordant voice profaned the holy calm, and a deluge of water drenched the prone martyr's remains!

The strangling hero sprang up with a relieving snort.

Not long after, as Tom, all undressed for bed, was surveying his drenched garments by the light of a tallow dip. He went to bed without the mandatory prayers.

Chapter 4

In the morning, Mary gave Tom a tin basin of water and a piece of soap, asking Tom to have a bath, but Tom poured out the water on the ground, gently, and then entered the kitchen and began to wipe his face diligently on the towel behind the door. But Mary removed the towel and said:

"Now ain't you ashamed, Tom. You mustn't be so bad. Water won't hurt you."

Then Mary took him in hand, and when she was done with him he was a man and a brother. His hair was neatly brushed. Then Mary got out a suit of his clothing. Then she crowned him with his speckled straw hat. Much against his wishes he had to wear his polished shoes.

Mary was soon ready, and the three children set out for Sunday-school—a place that Tom

*"Now ain't you ashamed, Tom.
Water won't hurt you," said Mary.*

hated with his whole heart; but Sid and Mary were fond of it.

At the door Tim dropped back a step and accosted a Sunday-dressed comrade and exchanged some playthings with him.

Tom traded a couple of white alleys for three red tickets. He waylaid other boys as they came, and went on buying tickets of various colors ten or fifteen minutes longer. He entered the church, now, with a swarm of clean and noisy boys and girls, proceeded to his seat and started a quarrel with the first boy that came handy. The boys teased each other.

However, they worried through, and each got his reward—in small blue tickets, each with a passage of Scripture on it. Anybody who had memorized two thusand verses got a Bible, but, in fact, only the older pupils managed to keep their tickets and stick to their tedious work long enough to get a Bible. It is possible that Tom's mental stomach had never really hungered for one of those prizes, but unquestionably his entire being had for many a day longed for the glory and the eclat that came with it.

In due course the superintendent stood up in front of the pulpit, with a closed hymn-book in his hand and his forefinger inserted between its leaves, and commanded attention.

Then came Thatcher, accompanied by a very feeble and aged man; a fine, portly, middle-aged gentleman with iron-gray hair; and a dignified lady who was doubtless the latter's wife. The lady was leading a child. Tom had been restless and full of chafings and repinings; conscience-smitten, too—he could not meet Amy Lawrence's eye, he could not brook her loving gaze. But when he saw this small newcomer his soul was all ablaze with bliss in a moment. The next moment he was "showing off" with all his might—cuffing boys, pulling hair, making faces.

The visitors were given the highest seat of honor, and as soon as Mr. Walters' speech was finished, he introduced them to the school. The middle-aged man turned out to be a prodigious personage—no less a one than the county judge—altogether the most august creation these children had ever looked upon. He was from Constantinople, twelve miles away—so he had travelled, and seen the world. This was the great Judge Thatcher, brother of their own lawyer. Jeff Thatcher immediately went forward, to be familiar with the great man and be envied by the school. Now, Mr. Walters the librarian, the teachers, in fact, everybody was showing off.

There was only one thing wanting to make Mr. Walters' ecstasy complete, and that was a chance to deliver a Bible-prize and exhibit a prodigy. Several pupils had a few yellow tickets, but none had enough—he had been around among the star pupils inquiring.

And now at this moment, when hope was dead, Tom Sawyer came forward with nine yellow tickets, nine red tickets, and ten blue ones, and demanded a Bible. This was a thunderbolt out of a clear sky. Tom was therefore elevated to a place with the Judge and the other elect, and the great news was announced from headquarters. It was the most stunning surprise of the decade. The boys were all eaten up with envy.

Amy Lawrence was proud and glad, and she tried to make Tom see it in her face—but he wouldn't look.

Tom was introduced to the Judge. The Judge asked him what his name was.

"Thomas Sawyer—sir," said Tom stammering.

"You'll be a great man and a good, mam yourself, some day, Thomas," said the Judge.

Chapter 5

About half-past ten the cracked bell of the small church began to ring, and presently the people began to gather for the morning sermon. The Sunday-school children distributed themselves about the house and occupied pews with their parents, so as to be under supervision. There were Aunt Polly, Tom, Sid and Mary. In the crowd there were also the aged and needy postmaster, the mayor and his wife; the justice of the peace; the widow Douglas, the bent and venerable Major and Mrs. Ward; lawyer Riverson, the belle of the village, followed by a troop of lawn-clad and ribbon-decked young heart-breakers; then all the young clerks in town in a body, a circling wall of oiled and simpering admirers and last of all came the Model Boy, Willie Mufferson, taking as heedful care of his mother as if she were cut glass. His white handkerchief was hanging out of his pocket behind, as usual on Sundays. Tom had no handkerchief, and he looked upon boys who had as snobs.

The congregation being fully assembled, the minister gave out the hymn, and read it through with a relish. His voice began on a medium key and climbed steadily up till it reached a certain point, where it bore with strong emphasis upon the topmost word and then plunged down as if from a spring-board.

After the hymn had been sung, the Rev. Mr. Sprague turned himself into a bulletin-board, and read off "notices" of meetings and societies and things till it seemed that the list would stretch out to the crack of doom—a queer custom which is still kept up in America.

Tom did not enjoy the prayer, he only endured it. He was restive all through it. In the midst of the prayer a fly had lit on the back of the pew in front of him and tortured his spirit. Tom's hands itched to grab for it but they did not dare-he believed his soul would be instantly destroyed if he did such a thing while the prayer was going on. But with the closing sentence his hand began to curve

His aunt detected the act and made him let the fly go.

and steal forward; and the instant the "Amen" was out the fly was a prisoner of war. His aunt detected the act and made him let it go.

The minister gave out his text and droned along monotonously through an argument that was so prosy that many a head by and by began to nod. Tom counted the pages of the sermon; after church he always knew how many pages there had been, but he seldom knew anything else about the discourse.

Now he lapsed into suffering again, as the dry argument was resumed. Presently he bethought him of a treasure he had and got it out. It was a large black beetle with formidable jaws—a "pinchbug," he called it. The beetle lay there working its helpless legs, unable to turn over. Tom eyed it, and longed for it; but it was safe out of his reach. Other people uninterested in the sermon found relief in the beetle, and they eyed it too. Presently a vagrant poodle dog came idling along, sad at heart, lazy with the summer softness and the quiet, weary of captivity, sighing for change. He spied the beetle; the drooping tail lifted and wagged. He surveyed the prize; walked around it; smelt at it from a safe distance; walked around it again; grew bolder, and took a closer smell; then lifted his lip and made a gingerly snatch at it, just missing it; made another, and another; began to enjoy the diversion; subsided to his stomach with the beetle between his paws, and continued his experiments; grew weary at last, and then indifferent and absent-minded.

Then there was a wild yelp of agony and the poodle went sailing up the aisle; the yelps continued, and so did the dog; he crossed the house in front of the altar; he flew down the other aisle; he crossed before the doors; he clamored up the home-stretch; his anguish grew with his progress, till presently he was but a woolly comet moving in its orbit with the gleam and the speed of light.

At last the frantic sufferer sheered from its course, and sprang into its master's lap; he flung it out of the window, and the voice of distress quickly thinned away.

By this time the whole church was red-faced and suffocating with suppressed laughter. It was a genuine relief to the whole congregation when the ordeal was over and the benediction pronounced.

Tom Sawyer went home quite cheerful, thinking to himself that there was some satisfaction about divine service when there was a bit of variety in it.

Chapter 6

Monday morning found Tom Sawyer miserable. Monday morning always found him so—because it began another week's slow suffering in school.

Tom lay thinking. Presently it occurred to him that he wished he was sick; then he could stay home from school. He canvassed his system. Suddenly he discovered something. One of his upper front teeth was loose. He was about to begin to groan, when it occurred to him that if he came into court with that argument, his aunt would pull it out, and that would hurt. So he thought he would hold the tooth in reserve for the present.

Then he remembered hearing the doctor tell about a certain thing that laid up a patient for two or three weeks. So the boy eagerly drew his sore toe from under the sheet and held it up for inspection. He fell to groaning with considerable spirit.

But Sid snored on.

He said, "Sid, Sid!" and shook him. This course worked well, and Tom began to groan again. Sid yawned, and began to stare at Tom. Tom went on groaning. Sid said:

"Tom! Say, Tom!" [No response.] "Here, Tom! TOM! What is the matter, Tom?" Tom told him that an awful pain in his foot was going to kill him.

Then Sid flew down-stairs and said:

"Oh, Aunt Polly, come! Tom's dying!"

She fled up-stairs, with Sid and Mary at her heels. When she reached the bedside she gasped out:

"Tom! Tom, what's the matter with you?"

"Oh, auntie, my sore toe's mortified!"

The old lady sank down into a chair and laughed a little.

The boy felt a little foolish, and he said:

"Aunt Polly, it SEEMED mortified, and it hurt so I never minded my tooth at all. "One of them's loose, and it aches perfectly awful."

"Open your mouth. Mary, get me a silk thread, and a chunk of fire out of the kitchen."

Tom said:

"Oh, please, auntie, don't pull it out. It don't hurt any more."

By this time the dental instruments were ready. The old lady made one end of the silk thread fast to Tom's tooth with a loop and tied the other to the bedpost. Then she seized the chunk of fire and suddenly thrust it almost into the boy's face. The tooth hung dangling by the bedpost, now.

As Tom wended to school after breakfast, he was the envy of every boy he met because the gap in his upper row of teeth enabled him to expectorate in a new and admirable way. So far, a boy who had cut his finger had been a centre of fascination. Now, Tom became the hero in his place among the boys.

Shortly Tom came upon the juvenile pariah of the village, Huckleberry Finn, son of the town drunkard. Huckleberry was cordially hated and dreaded by all the mothers of the town, because he was idle and lawless and vulgar and bad—and because all their children admired him so, and delighted in his forbidden society, and wished they dared to be like him. Tom was like the rest of the respectable boys, in that he envied Huckleberry his gaudy outcast condition, and was under strict orders not to play with him. But he played with him every time he got a chance. Huckleberry was always dressed in the cast-off clothes of full-grown men, and they were in perennial bloom and fluttering with rags.

Huckleberry came and went, at his own free will. He did whatever he liked and there was no check in his activities. He never had to wash, nor put on clean clothes.

Tom hailed the romantic outcast:

"Hello, Huckleberry!"

"What's that you got?"

"Dead cat."

Where'd you get him?"

"Bought him off'n a boy."

"Say—what is dead cats good for, Huck?"

"Good for? Cure warts with."

Then there was a discussion on different methods of curing warts. These methods included the use of spunk water as well as a dead cat.

Tom and Huckleberry Finn happy in each other's company.

Then the boys exchanged their precious possessions. Tom got a tick by exchaging his extracted tooth for it.

Tom enclosed the tick in the percussion-cap box that had lately been the pinchbug's prison.

Then Tom went to the little isolated frame schoolhouse. The master, throned on high in his great splint-bottom arm-chair, was dozing. The interruption roused him.

"Thomas Sawyer!" Come up here. Now, sir, why are you late again, as usual?"

Tom instantly said:

"I STOPPED TO TALK WITH HUCKLEBERRY FINN!"

The master said:

"Thomas Sawyer, this is the most astounding confession I have ever listened to. Take off your jacket."

The master's arm performed until it was tired. Then the order followed:

"Now, sir, go and sit with the girls! And let this be a warning to you."

He sat down upon the end of the pine bench and the girl hitched herself away from him with a toss of her head.

He gave her advances step by step and finally won her. First of all, he offered her a peach. She refused to take it. Then he made a drawing on the slate which she appreciated. She wanted to learn drawing.

"It's easy," whispered Tom, "I'll learn you."

"Good—that's a whack, "said Tom, "What's your name?" said Tom.

"Becky Thatcher. What's yours?"

"You call me Tom, will you?"

"Yes."

Now Tom began to scrawl something on the slate. It was "I LOVE YOU."

"Oh, you bad thing!" And she hit his hand a smart rap, but reddened and looked pleased, nevertheless.

Just at this juncture the boy felt a slow, fateful grip closing on his ear, and a steady lifting impulse. In that wise he was borne across the house and deposited in his own seat under a peppering fire of giggles from the whole school. Then the master stood over him during a few awful moments, and finally moved away.

As the school quieted down Tome made an honest effort to study, but the turmoil within him was too great.

Chapter 7

The harder Tom tried to fasten his mind on his book, the more his ideas wandered. His heart ached to be free. His hand wandered into his pocket. Then furtively the percussion-cap box came out. He released the tick and put him on the long flat desk.

Tom's bosom friend sat next him, suffering just as Tom had been, and now he was deeply interested in this entertainment in an instant. This bosom friend was Joe Harper.

Then Tom put Joe's slate on the desk and drew a line down the middle of it from top to bottom.

"Now," said he, "as long as he is on your side you can stir him up and I'll let him alone; but if you let him get away and get on my side, you're to leave him alone as long as I can keep him from crossing over."

The creature moved sides frequently. But soon the two boys indulged in a war of words violently.

Just then, a tremendous whack came down on Tom's shoulders, and its duplicate on Joe's. It was master's.

When school broke up at noon, Tom flew to Becky Thatcher, and whispered in her ear to go home ostensibly but come back to him, giving a slip to others.

As she came, they sat together, with a slate before them, and Tom gave Becky the pencil and held her hand in his, guiding it. Tom asked her if she loved dead rats. She said that she hated them.

"What I like is chewing-gum," she said "I've got some. I'll let you chew it awhile, but you must give it back to me."

That was agreeable, so they chewed it turn about, and dangled their legs against the bench in excess of contentment.

Then in a very clever way Tom made her whisper in his ear, "I Love You."

Then she sprang away and ran around and around the desks and benches, with Tom after

As Tom named Amy Lawrence, the girl began to cry.

her, and took refuge in a corner at last, with her little white apron to her face. Tom clasped her about her neck and succeeded in kissing her red lips.

Then both of them promised each other that they would not love and marry anybody except each other.

As by chance the name of Amy Lawrence slipped from Tom's mouth, the child began to cry. Despite all efforts of Tom, she did not stop crying. Then his pride was up, and he strode away and went outside. He stood about, restless and uneasy, for a while, hoping she would repent and come to find him. But she did not. Then Tom's heart smote him. He went to her and tried to soothe her agitated mind, but she continued sobbing.

He tried to lure her by giving her a brass knob from the top of an andiron, but in vain.

Then Tom marched out of the house and over the hills and far away, to return to school no more that day. Presently Becky began to suspect. She ran to the door; he was not in sight.

"Tom! Come back, Tom!"

She listened intently, but there was no answer. So she sat down to cry again and upbraid herself, and by this time the scholars began to gather again, and she had to hide her griefs and still her broken heart and take up the cross of a long, dreary, aching afternoon, with none among the strangers about her to exchange sorrow with.

Chapter 8

Tom dodged hither and thither through lanes until he was well out of the track of returning scholars, and then fell into a moody jog. He crossed a small "branch" two or three times, because of a prevailing juvenile superstition that to cross water baffled pursuit. Half an hour later he was disappearing behind the Douglas mansion on the summit of Cardiff Hill. He entered a dense wood, and began to meditate. He was sad though the atmosphere was happy and peaceful. Now as to this girl. What had he done? Nothing. She would be sorry some day—maybe when it was too late. Ah, if he could only die TEMPORARILY!

What if he turned his back, now, and disappeared mysteriously? How would she feel then! He thought about becoming a soldier or a hunting Indian chief, but finally decided to be a pirate. He began to imagine what a fearful gaudy pirate he would be!

Yes, it was settled. He would run away from home and enter upon it. He would start the very next morning. Therefore he must now begin to get ready. He would collect his resources together. He went to a rotten log near at hand and began to dig under one end of it with his Barlow knife. He soon struck wood that sounded hollow.

Just here the blast of a toy tin trumpet came faintly down the green aisles of the forest. Tom flung off his jacket and trousers and got prepared, disclosing a rude bow and arrow, a lath sword and a tin trumpet, and in a moment had seized these things and bounded away, barelegged, with fluttering shirt. He presently halted under a great elm, blew an answering blast, and then began to tiptoe and look warily out, this way and that. He said cautiously—to an imaginary company:

"Hold, my merry men! Keep hid till I blow."

Now appeared Joe Harper, as airily clad and elaborately armed as Tom. Tom posing to be Robin Hood, called:

Tom dressed as Robin Hood and Joe as Guy of Guisborne in the imaginary Sherwood Forest.

"Hold! Who comes here into Sherwood Forest without my pass?"

"Guy of Guisborne wants no man's pass."

Then they took their lath swords, dumped their other traps on the ground, struck a fencing attitude, foot to foot, and began a grave, careful combat, "two up and two down."

So they "went it lively," panting and perspiring with the work. By and by Tom shouted:

"Fall! fall! Why don't you fall?"

"I sha'n't! Why don't you fall yourself?"

"Why, that ain't anything. I can't fall; that ain't the way it is in the book. The book says, 'Then with one back-handed stroke he slew poor Guy of Guisborne.' You're to turn around and let me hit you in the back."

There was no getting around the authorities, so Joe turned, received the whack and fell.

"Now," said Joe, getting up, "you got to let me kill YOU. That's fair."

"Why, I can't do that, it ain't in the book."

So the two boys enacted the whole life of Robin Hood upto his death.

Then the boys dressed themselves, hid their accoutrements, and went off grieving that there were no outlaws any more. They said they would rather be outlaws a year in Sherwood Forest than President of the United States forever.

Chapter 9

Tom and Sid were sent to bed, as usual. When it seemed to Tom that it must be nearly daylight, he heard the cry of "Scat! you devil!" and the crash of an empty bottle against the back of his aunt's woodshed. A single minute later he was dressed and out of the window. Huckleberry Finn was there, with his dead cat. The boys moved off wading through the tall grass of the graveyard.

It was a graveyard of the old-fashioned Western kind. It was on a hill, about a mile and a half from the village. It had a crazy board fence around it.

A faint wind moaned through the trees, and Tom feared it might be the spirits of the dead, complaining at being disturbed. The boys talked little, and only under their breath.

Then the boys heard some sounds.

Some vague figures approached through the gloom, swinging an old-fashioned tin lantern. Presently Huckleberry whispered with a shudder:

"It's the devils sure enough. Three of 'em! Lordy, Tom, we're goners! Can you pray?"

"I'll try, but don't you be afeard."

Then Huck said, "They're HUMANS! One of 'em is, anyway. One of 'em's old Muff Potter's voice."

"Huck I known another o' them voices; it's Injun Joe."

Now the three men had reached the grave and stood within a few feet of the boys' hiding-place.

"Here it is," said the third voice; and the owner of it held the lantern up and revealed the face of young Doctor Robinson.

Potter and Injun Joe were carrying a hand-barrow with a rope and a couple of shovels on it. They cast down their load and began to open the grave. The doctor put the lantern at the head of the grave and came and sat down with his back against one of the elm trees.

They went on digging. Finally a spade struck upon the coffin and within another minute or two the men had hoisted it out on the ground. They pried off the lid with their shovels, got out the body and dumped it rudely on the ground. The barrow was got ready and the corpse placed on it, covered with a blanket, and bound to its place with the rope. Potter took out a large spring-knife and cut off the dangling end of the rope and then said:

"Now the cussed thing's ready, Sawbones, and you'll just out with another five, or here she stays."

"That's the talk!" said Injun Joe.

"Look here, what does this mean?" said the doctor. "You required your pay in advance, and I've paid you."

"Yes, and you done more than that," said Injun Joe, approaching the doctor, who was now standing. "Five years ago you drove me away from your father's kitchen one night, when I come to ask for something to eat, and you said I warn't there for any good; and when I swore I'd get even with you if it took a hundred years, your father had me jailed for a vagrant. Did you think I'd forget? The Injun blood ain't in me for nothing. And now I've GOT you, and you got to SETTLE, you know!"

He was threatening the doctor, with his fist in his face. The doctor struck out suddenly and stretched the ruffian on the ground. Potter dropped his knife, and exclaimed:

"Here, now, don't you hit my pard!" and the next moment he had grappled with the doctor and the two were struggling with might and main. Injun Joe sprang to his feet, snatched up Potter's knife, and went creeping, round and round about the combatants. All at once the doctor flung himself free, seized the heavy headboard of Williams' grave and felled Potter to the earth with it—and in the same instant the half-breed saw his chance and drove the knife to the hilt in the young man's breast. He reeled and fell partly upon Potter flooding him with his blood, and the two frightened boys went speeding away in the dark.

Presently, Injun Joe was standing over the two forms, contemplating them. The doctor murmured inarticulately, gave a long gasp or two and was still. The half-breed muttered:

"THAT score is settled—damn you."

*"Joe, I never meant to—'pon my soul and honour"
pleaded Potter with Joe.*

Then he robbed the body. After which he put the fatal knife in Potter's open right hand, and sat down on the dismantled coffin. Three—four—five minutes passed, and then Potter began to stir and moan. His hand closed upon the knife; he raised it, glanced at it, and let it fall, with a shudder. Then he sat up, pushing the body from him, and gazed at it, and then around him, confusedly. His eyes met Joe's.

Then Potter explained to Joe: Joe, I never meant to—'pon my soul and honor, I never meant to, Joe.

"Oh, I didn't know what I was a-doing. I wish I may die this minute if I did. It was all on account of the whiskey and the excitement, I reckon. I never used a weapon in my life before, Joe."

"No, you've always been fair and square with me, Muff Potter, and I won't go back on you. There, now, that's as fair as a man can say."

"Oh, Joe, you're an angel. I'll bless you for this the longest day I live." And Potter began to cry.

"Come, now, that's enough of that. This ain't any time for blubbering. You be off yonder way and I'll go this. Move, now, and don't leave any tracks behind you."

Two or three minutes later the murdered man, the blanketed corpse, the lidless coffin, and the open grave were under no inspection but the moon's. The stillness was complete again, too.

Chapter 10

The two boys flew on and on, toward the village, speechless with horror. They glanced backward over their shoulders from time to time, apprehensively, as if they feared they might be followed.

"If we can only get to the old tannery before we break down!" whispered Tom, in short catches between breaths."

Huckleberry's hard pantings were his only reply.

The boys whispered to each other about what could happen to them. They feared that Injun Joe might kill them, unless he is hanged for killing Doctor Robinson if the latter dies. At last, they decide to keep mum.

To honour this agreement they signed a contract in blood, drawn from their thumbs. The contract idea was that of Tom. Its language was written by Tom and was appreciated by Huck.

A figure crept stealthily through a break in the other end of the ruined building, now, but they did not notice it.

Presently a dog set up a long, lugubrious howl just outside.

Tom pricked up his ears.

"Sh! What's that?" he whispered.

"Sounds like—like hogs grunting. No—it's somebody snoring, Tom."

The spirit of adventure rose in the boys' souls once more.

They started tiptoeing stealthily. When they had got to within five steps of the snorer, Tom stepped on a stick, and it broke with a sharp snap. The man moaned, writhed a little, and his face came into the moonlight. It was Muff Potter. The boys' hearts had stood still. They tiptoed out, through the broken weather-boarding, and stopped at a little distance to exchange a parting word.

The dog howled again standing within a few feet of where Potter was lying. The boys

She wept over him and asked him how he could go and break her heart so.

believed that soon Potter would be no more, as per an old superstition of negroes.

Then they separated, cogitating. When Tom crept in at his bedroom window the night was almost spent. He undressed with excessive caution, and fell asleep congratulating himself that nobody knew of his escapade. He was not aware that the gently-snoring Sid was awake, and had been so for an hour. When Tom awoke, Sid was dressed and gone. Within five minutes he was dressed and down-stairs, feeling sore and drowsy. The family were still at table, but they had finished breakfast.

After breakfast his aunt took him aside. She wept over him and asked him how he could go and break her old heart so. This was worse than a thousand whippings, and Tom's heart was sorer now than his body. He cried, he pleaded for forgiveness, promised to reform over and over again.

He moped to school gloomy and sad, and took his flogging, along with Joe Harper, for playing hookey the day before.

He was awfully sad when he found at his desk his elbow pressing against some hard substance. He slowly and sadly took up this object with a sigh. It was in a paper. He unrolled it. A long, lingering, colossal sigh followed, and his heart broke. It was his brass andiron knob!

This final feather broke the camel's back.

Chapter 11

Close upon the hour of noon the whole village was suddenly electrified with the ghastly news.

A gory knife had been found close to the murdered man, and it had been recognized by somebody as belonging to Muff Potter. It was also said that the town had been ransacked for this "murderer" but that he could not be found.

All the town was drifting toward the graveyard. Tom's heartbreak vanished and he joined the procession. There his eyes met Huckleberry's.

People were talking about the murder and believed Muff Potter to be the murderer.

Now Tom shivered from head to heel; for his eye fell upon the stolid face of Injun Joe. At this moment the crowd began to sway and struggle as they saw Muff Potter.

The crowd fell apart, now, and the Sheriff came through, ostentatiously leading Potter by the arm. The poor fellow's face was haggard, and his eyes showed the fear that was upon him.

"I didn't do it, friends," he sobbed; "'pon my word and honor I never done it."

He saw Injun Joe, and exclaimed:

"Oh, Injun Joe, you promised me you'd never..."

"Is that your knife?" and it was thrust before him by the Sheriff.

Then Huckleberry and Tom stood dumb and staring.

Injun Joe helped to raise the body of the murdered man and put it in a wagon for removal. The boys thought that Joe would at last come under suspicion; but they were disappointed, for more than one villager remarked:

"It was within three feet of Muff Potter when it done it."

Tom's fearful secret and gnawing conscience disturbed his sleep for as much as a week after this; and he talked in his sleep. It was noticed by both Sid and Aunt Polly.

On being asked, Tom said, "Nothing. Nothing 't I know of." But the boy's hand shook so that he spilled his coffee.

At last Aunt Polly said:

"Sho! It's that dreadful murder. I dream about it most every night myself. Sometimes I dream it's me that done it."

So, the matter was dismissed for the time being. But, Sid, secretly kept a strict watch over Tom's sleeping habits, and even at school Tom's behavior showed a remarkable change. Tom was no longer aggressive or interfering.

The villagers had a strong desire to tar-and-feather Injun Joe and ride him on a rail, for body-snatching, but so formidable was his character that nobody could be found who was willing to take the lead in the matter, so it was dropped. He had been careful to begin both of his inquest-statements with the fight, without confessing the grave-robbery that preceded it; therefore it was deemed wisest not to try the case in the courts at present.

Chapter 12

Becky Thatcher had stopped coming to school. She was ill. What if she should die! He no longer took an interest in war, nor even in piracy. His aunt was concerned. She began to try all manner of remedies on him.

The water treatment was new, now, and she had him out at daylight every morning, stood him up in the woodshed and drowned him with a deluge of cold water. She added hot baths, sitz baths, shower baths, and plunges.

Tom had become indifferent to persecution by this time. This phase filled the old lady's heart with consternation. This indifference must be broken up at any cost. Now she heard of Pain-killer for the first time, and pinned her faith to Pain-killer. Her troubles were instantly at rest, her soul at peace again; for the "indifference" was broken up. The boy could not have shown a wilder, heartier interest, if she had built a fire under him.

Tom felt that it was time to wake up. So he thought over various plans for relief, and finally hit pon that of professing to be fond of Pain-killer. He asked for it so often that he became a nuisance. She found that the medicine did really diminish, but it did not occur to her that the boy was mending the health of a crack in the sitting-room floor with it.

One day Tom was in the act of dosing the crack when his aunt's yellow cat, Peter, came along, purring, eying the teaspoon avariciously, and begging for a taste.

After some hesitation so Tom pried his mouth open and poured down the Pain-killer. Peter sprang a couple of yards in the air, and then delivered a war-whoop and set off round and round the room, banging against furniture, upsetting flower-pots, and making general havoc. Aunt Polly entered in time to see him throw a few double summersets, deliver a final mighty hurrah, and sail through the open window, carrying the rest of the flower-pots with him. Tom lay on the floor expiring with laughter.

Tom pried the cat's mouth open and poured down the pain-killer

The old lady was bending down. The handle of the telltale teaspoon was visible under the bed-valance. Aunt Polly took it, held it up. Tom winced, and dropped his eyes. Aunt Polly raised him by the usual handle—his ear—and cracked his head soundly with her thimble.

"Now, sir, what did you want to treat that poor dumb beast so, for?"

"I done it out of pity for him—because he hadn't any aunt," Tom replied

She began to soften; and said to Tom:

"Tom, you needn't take any more medicine."

Tom reached school ahead of time. It was noticed that this strange thing had been occurring every day latterly. And now, as usual of late, he hung about the gate of the schoolyard instead of playing with his comrades.

Tom watched and watched, looking at frocks, but in vain. Then one more frock passed in at the gate. The next instant he was out. He carried his exploits to her immediate vicinity; broke through a group of boys, tumbling them in every direction, and fell sprawling, himself, under Becky's nose,— and she turned, with her nose in the air, and he heard her say: "Mf! some people think they're mighty smart—always showing off!"

Tom's cheeks burned. He gathered himself up and sneaked off, crushed and crestfallen.

Chapter 13

Tom's mind was made up now. He was gloomy and desperate. He was a forsaken, friendless boy, he said; nobody loved him. He would lead a life of crime. There was no choice.

He decided to stop going to school. Just at this point he met his soul's sworn comrade, Joe Harper. He wanted to escape from hard usage and lack of sympathy at home by roaming abroad into the great world never to return.

But it transpired that this was a request which Joe had just been going to make of Tom, and had come to hunt him up for that purpose.

The two friends resolved never to separate till death. Joe wanted to be a hermit, but Tom convinced him to be a pirate instead and lead a life of crime.

They chose Jackson's Island which was unhabitated. Then they hunted up Huckleberry

Tom hailing Huck and Joe on the river-bank at midnight.

Finn, and he joined them promptly. They presently separated to meet at a lonely spot on the river-bank two miles above the village at the favorite hour—which was midnight.

About midnight Tom arrived with a boiled ham and a few trifles. Then he gave a low, distinct whistle. It was answered from under the bluff. Tom whistled twice more; these signals were answered in the same way. Then a guarded voice said:

"Who goes there?"

"Tom Sawyer, the Black Avenger of the Spanish Main. Name your names."

"Huck Finn the Red-Handed, and Joe Harper the Terror of the Seas." Tom had furnished these titles, from his favorite literature. "Tis well. Give the countersign."

Two hoarse whispers delivered the same awful word simultaneously to the brooding night:

"BLOOD!"

The Terror of the Seas had brought a side of bacon. Finn the Red-Handed had stolen a skillet and a quantity of half-cured leaf tobacco, and had also brought a few corn-cobs to make pipes with. But none of the pirates smoked or "chewed" but himself. The Black Avenger of the Spanish Main said it would never do to start without some fire. That was a wise thought; matches were hardly known there in that day.

They saw a fire smouldering upon a great raft a hundred yards above, and they went stealthily thither and helped themselves to a chunk. They made an imposing adventure of it, saying, "Hist!" every now and then, and suddenly halting with finger on lip; moving with hands on imaginary dagger-hilts; and giving orders in dismal whispers that if "the foe" stirred, to "let him have it to the hilt," because "dead men tell no tales."

They shoved off, presently, Tom in command, Huck at the after oar and Joe at the forward. As the boys steadily and monotonously drove the raft toward mid-stream it was no doubt understood that these orders were given only for "style," and were not intended to mean anything in particular.

"What sail's she carrying?"

"Courses, tops'ls, and flying-jib, sir."

"Send the r'yals up! Lay out aloft, there, half a dozen of ye—foretopmaststuns'l! Lively, now!"

"Aye-aye, sir!"

"Shake out that maintogalans'l! Sheets and braces! NOW my hearties!"

"Aye-aye, sir!"

"Hellum-a-lee—hard a port! Stand by to meet her when she comes! Port, port! NOW, men! With a will! Stead-y-y-y!"

"Steady it is, sir!"

The raft drew beyond the middle of the river; the boys pointed her head right, and then lay on their oars. About two o'clock in the morning the raft grounded on the bar two hundred yards above the head of the island, and they waded back and forth until they had landed their freight. Part of the little raft's belongings consisted of an old sail, and this they spread over a nook in the bushes for a tent to shelter their provisions; but they themselves would sleep in the open air in good weather, as became outlaws.

They built a fire against the side of a great log twenty or thirty steps within the sombre depths of the forest, and then cooked some bacon in the frying-pan for supper, and used up half of the corn "pone" stock they had brought.

It seemed glorious sport to be feasting in that wild, free way in the virgin forest of an unexplored and uninhabited island, far from the haunts of men, and they said they never would return to civilization.

It seemed glorious to be feasting in that wild, virgin forest.

When the last crisp slice of bacon was gone, and the last allowance of corn pone devoured, the boys stretched themselves out on the grass, filled with contentment. They could have found a cooler place, but they would not deny themselves such a romantic feature as the roasting camp-fire.

"It's just the life for me," said Tom. "You don't have to get up, mornings, and you don't have to go to school, and wash, and all that blame foolishness. You see a pirate don't have to do ANYTHING, Joe, when he's ashore, but a hermit HE has to be praying considerable, and then he don't have any fun, anyway, all by himself that way."

"Oh yes, that's so," said Joe, "but I hadn't thought much about it, you know. I'd a good deal rather be a pirate, now that I've tried it."

Presently Huck said:

"What does pirates have to do?"

Tom said:

"Oh, they have just a bully time—take ships and burn them, and get the money and bury it in awful places in their island where there's ghosts and things to watch it, and kill everybody in the ships—make 'em walk a plank."

"And they carry the women to the island," said Joe; "they don't kill the women."

"No," assented Tom, "they don't kill the women—they're too noble. And the women's always beautiful, too."

"And don't they wear the bulliest clothes! Oh no! All gold and silver and di'monds," said Joe, with enthusiasm.

"Who?" said Huck.

"Why, the pirates."

Huck scanned his own clothing forlornly.

"I reckon I ain't dressed fitten for a pirate," said he, with a regretful pathos in his voice; "but I ain't got none but these."

But the other boys told him the fine clothes would come fast enough, after they should have begun their adventures. They made him understand that his poor rags would do to begin with, though it was customary for wealthy pirates to start with a proper wardrobe.

Gradually their talk died out and drowsiness began to steal upon the eyelids of the little waifs, and these curiously inconsistent pirates feel peacefully to sleep.

Chapter 14

When Tom awoke in the morning, he wondered where he was. Then he comprehended. He stirred up the other pirates and they all clattered away with a shout, and in a minute or two were stripped and chasing after and tumbling over each other in the shallow limpid water of the white sandbar.

They came back to camp wonderfully refreshed, glad-hearted, and ravenous; and they soon had the camp-fire blazing up again. While Joe was slicing bacon for breakfast, Tom and Huck asked him to hold on a minute; they stepped to a promising nook in the riverbank and threw in their lines; almost immediately they had reward of some wonderful fish. They fried the fish with the bacon, and were astonished; for no fish had ever seemed so delicious before.

They lay around in the shade, after breakfast, while Huck had a smoke, and then went off through the woods on an exploring expedition.

They took a swim about every hour, so it was close upon the middle of the afternoon when they got back to camp. They were too hungry to stop to fish, but they fared sumptuously upon cold ham, and then threw themselves down in the shade to talk. But the talk soon began to drag, and then died. A sort of undefined longing crept upon them. This took dim shape, presently—it was budding homesickness.

For some time, now, the boys had been dully conscious of a peculiar sound in the distance. But now this mysterious sound became more pronounced.

They decided to go and see.

They saw a little steam ferryboat about a mile below the village, drifting with the current. Her broad deck seemed crowded with people. Presently a great jet of white smoke burst from the ferryboat's side, and as it expanded and rose in a lazy cloud, that same dull throb of sound was borne to the listeners again.

They saw a little steam ferryboat drifting with the current.

"I know now!" exclaimed Tom; "somebody's drownded!"

Then Tom exclaimed:

"Boys, I know who's drownded—it's us!"

They felt like heroes in an instant. This was fine. It was worth while to be a pirate, after all.

As twilight drew on, the ferryboat went back to her accustomed business and the skiffs disappeared. The pirates returned to camp. They were jubilant with vanity over their new grandeur and the illustrious trouble they were making.

As the night deepened, Huck began to nod, and presently to snore. Joe followed next. Tom got up cautiously. He picked up and inspected several large semi-cylinders of the thin white bark of a sycamore. Then he knelt by the fire and painfully wrote something upon each of these with his "red keel"; one he rolled up and put in his jacket pocket, and the other he put in Joe's hat and removed it to a little distance from the owner.

And he also put into the hat certain schoolboy treasures of almost inestimable value—among them a lump of chalk, an India-rubber ball, three fishhooks, and one of that kind of marbles known as a "sure 'nough crystal." Then he tiptoed his way cautiously among the trees till he felt that he was out of hearing, and straightway broke into a keen run in the direction of the sandbar.

Chapter 15

A few minutes later Tom was in the shoal water of the bar, wading toward the Illinois shore. Partly swimming and partly applying strokes to the skiff, he reached the village.

He flew along unfrequented alleys, and shortly found himself at his aunt's back fence. He climbed over, approached the "ell," and looked in at the sitting-room window. There sat Aunt Polly, Sid, Mary, and Joe Harper's mother, grouped together, talking. Tom went to the door and began to softly lift the latch; then he pressed gently and continued pushing cautiously, till he judged he might squeeze through on his knees; so he put his head through and began, warily.

As aunt Polly asked Sid to go and shut the door, Tom disappeared under the bed just in time. He lay and then crept to where he could almost touch his aunt's foot.

"But as I was saying," said Aunt Polly, "he warn't BAD, so to say —only mischEEvous — and she began to cry.

"It was just so with my Joe—always full of his devilment, and up to every kind of mischief, but he was just as unselfish and kind as he could be—Mrs. Harper sobbed as if her heart would break.

Tom was listening all the good words about himself and he was sufficiently touched by his aunt's grief to long to rush out from under the bed and overwhelm her with joy, but he resisted and lay still.

It was conjectured at first that the boys had got drowned while taking a swim; then the small raft had been missed; next, certain boys said the missing lads had promised that the village should "hear something" soon; the wiseheads had "put this and that together" and decided that the lads had gone off on that raft and would turn up at next town below, presently; but toward noon the raft had been found, lodged against the Missouri shore some five or six miles below the village-and then hope perished. This was Wednesday night. Finally, it was decided that if the bodies

Tom with Joe and Huck.

continued missing until Sunday, all hope would be given over, and the funerals would be preached on that morning. Tom shuddered.

Aunt Polly knelt down and prayed for Tom so touchingly, so appealingly, and with such measureless love in her words and her old trembling voice, that he was weltering in tears again, long before she was through.

At last she was still, only moaning a little in her sleep. Now the boy stole out, rose gradually by the bedside, shaded the candle-light with his hand, and stood regarding her. His heart was full of pity for her. He took out his sycamore scroll and placed it by the candle. But something occurred to him, and he lingered considering. He put the bark hastily in his pocket. Then he bent over and kissed the faded lips, and straightway made his stealthy exit, latching the door behind him.

He threaded his way back to the ferry landing, and was soon rowing cautiously upstream. He hit the landing on the other side neatly, stepped ashore and entered the woods.

A little later he paused, dripping, upon the threshold of the camp, and heard Joe and Huck talking about him.

Suddenly Tom made his grand presence into camp. He recounted (and adorned) his adventures. They were a vain and boastful company of heroes when the tale was done. Then Tom hid himself away in a shady nook to sleep till noon, and the other pirates got ready to fish and explore.

Chapter 16

After dinner all the gang turned out to hunt for turtle eggs on the bar. They had a famous fried-egg feast that night, and another on Friday morning.

After breakfast they went whooping and prancing out on the bar, and chased each other round and round, shedding clothes as they went, until they were naked. And now and then they stooped in a group and splashed water in each other's faces with their palms.

When they were well exhausted, they would run out and sprawl on the dry, hot sand, and lie there and cover themselves up with it, and by and by break for the water again and go through the original performance once more.

Next they got their marbles and played "knucks" and "ring-taw" and "keeps" till that amusement grew stale. They gradually wandered apart, dropped into the "dumps," and fell to gazing longingly across the wide river to where the village lay drowsing in the sun.

Then Tom found himself writing "BECKY" in the sand with his big toe; he scratched it out, and was angry with himself for his weakness. But he wrote it again, nevertheless; he could not help it. He erased it once more and then took himself out of temptation by driving the other boys together and joining them.

But now Joe was so homesick that he could hardly endure the misery of it. Huck was melancholy, too. Tom was downhearted, but tried hard not to show it.

Then Joe openly declared that he was homesick and waited to see his mother. Finally he said:

"Oh, boys, let's give it up. I want to go home. It's so lonesome."

"Oh no, Joe, you'll feel better by and by," said Tom. "Just think of the fishing that's here."

"I don't care for fishing. I want to go home."

As Joe moved moodily away and began to dress himself, Tom said, "We'll stay, won't we,

Huck? Let him go if he wants to. I reckon we can get along without him, per'aps."

Soon Huck also declared that he too wanted to go. He invited Tom also with him, but Tom said that he would better stay.

Presently, without a parting word, Joe began to wade off toward the Illinois shore. Tom's heart began to sink. He glanced at Huck.

Then Huck started sorrowfully away, and Tom stood looking after him, with a strong desire tugging at his heart to yield his pride and go along too. He made one final struggle with his pride, and then darted after his comrades, yelling:

"Wait! Wait! I want to tell you something!"

They presently stopped and turned around. Then Tom revealed to them his secret and the lads came gayly back and went at their sports again with a will, chattering all the time about Tom's stupendous plan and admiring the genius of it. After a dainty egg and fish dinner, Tom said he wanted to learn to smoke, now. Joe caught at the idea and said he would like to try, too. So Huck made pipes and filled them.

*Tom revealed to them his secret and
the lads came gayly back.*

Now they stretched themselves out on their elbows and began to puff.

"Why, many a time I've looked at people smoking, and thought well I wish I could do that; but I never thought I could," said Tom.

"I bleeve I could smoke this pipe all day," said Joe. "I don't feel sick."

"Neither do I," said Tom. "I could smoke it all day. But I bet you Jeff Thatcher couldn't."

So the talk ran on. But presently it began to flag a trifle, and grow disjointed. Every pore inside the boys' cheeks became a spouting fountain; little overflowings down their throats occurred in spite of all they could do, and sudden retchings followed every time. Both boys were looking very pale. Joe's pipe dropped from his nerveless fingers. Tom's followed.

They were not talkative at supper that night. They had a humble look.

About midnight Joe awoke, and called the boys. They found the atmosphere turbulent. There were deep peals of thundering preceded by frequent of lightning.

Presently there came a quivering glow that vaguely revealed the foliage for a moment and then vanished. By and by another came, a little stronger. Then another. Now a weird flash turned night into day and showed every little grass-blade, separate and distinct, that grew about their feet. And it showed three white, startled faces, too.

A deep peal of thunder went rolling and tumbling down the heavens and lost itself in sullen rumblings in the distance. Another fierce glare lit up the forest and an instant crash followed that seemed to rend the tree-tops right over the boys' heads. They clung together in terror, in the thick gloom that followed. A few big rain-drops fell pattering upon the leaves. It soon started raining heavily.

The boys rushed for the tent.

One by one they straggled in at last and took shelter under the tent, cold, scared, and streaming with water. The tempest rose higher and higher, and presently the sail tore loose from its fastenings and went winging away on the blast. The boys seized each others' hands and fled, with many tumblings and bruises, to the shelter of a great oak that stood upon the river-bank. Now the battle was at its highest. Under the ceaseless conflagration of lightning that flamed in the skies, everything below stood out in clean-cut and shadowless distinctness.

But at last the battle was done, and the forces retired with weaker and weaker threatenings and grumblings, and peace resumed her sway. The boys went back to camp.

Everything in camp was drenched, the

camp-fire as well. They piled on great dead boughs till they had a roaring furnace, and were glad-hearted once more. They dried their boiled ham and had a feast, and after that they sat by the fire and expanded and glorified their midnight adventure until morning, for there was not a dry spot to sleep on, anywhere around.

As the sun began to steal in upon the boys, drowsiness came over them. Tom found the boys homesick again.

He reminded them of the imposing secret, and raised a ray of cheer. While it lasted, he got them interested in a new device. This was to knock off being pirates, for a while, and be Indians for a change. They were attracted by this idea; so it was not long before they were stripped, and striped from head to heel with black mud, like so many zebras—all of them chiefs, of course—and then they went tearing through the woods to attack an English settlement.

By and by they separated into three hostile tribes, and darted upon each other from ambush with dreadful war-whoops, and killed and scalped each other by thousands. It was a gory day. Consequently it was an extremely satisfactory one.

They assembled in camp toward suppertime, hungry and happy; but now a difficulty arose—hostile Indians could not break the bread of hospitality together without first making peace, and this was a simple impossibility without smoking a pipe of peace. There was no other process that ever they had heard of. Two of the savages almost wished they had remained pirates. However, there was no other way; so with such show of cheerfulness as they could muster they called for the pipe and took their whiff as it passed, in due form.

And behold, they were glad they had gone into savagery, for they had gained something; they found that they could now smoke a little without having to go and hunt for a lost knife; they did not get sick enough to be seriously uncomfortable. They were not likely to fool away this high promise for lack of effort. No, they practised cautiously, after supper, with right fair success, and so they spent a jubilant evening.

Chapter 17

It was Saturday, but there was no hilarity in the little town. The Harpers, and Aunt Polly's family, were being put into mourning. The Saturday holiday seemed a burden to the children. They had no heart in their sports.

In the afternoon Becky Thatcher found herself moping about the deserted schoolhouse yard, and feeling very melancholy. She wished if she only had a brass and iron-knob again!

She said to herself:

"But he's gone now; I'll never, never, never see him any more."

This thought broke her down, and she wandered away, with tears rolling down her cheeks. Then quite a group of boys and girls—playmates of Tom's and Joe's—came by, and started talking about their wild pranks.

The three dead boys came marching up the aisle.

When the Sunday-school hour was finished, the next morning, the bell began to toll, instead of ringing in the usual way. It was a very still Sabbath, and the mournful sound seemed in keeping with the musing hush that lay upon nature. The villagers began to gather, and a touching mourning prayer and ceremony was held in the village church.

The minister related many a touching incident in the lives of the departed, which illustrated their sweet, generous natures. The congregation became more and more moved, till at last the whole company broke down the preacher himself giving way to his feelings, and crying in the pulpit.

There was a rustle in the gallery. A moment later the church door creaked. First one and then another pair of eyes followed the minister's, and then almost with one impulse the congregation rose and stared while the three dead boys came marching up the aisle, Tom in the lead, Joe next, and Huck, a ruin of drooping rags, sneaking sheepishly in the rear! They had been hid in the unused gallery listening to their own funeral sermon!

Aunt Polly, Mary, and the Harpers threw themselves upon their restored ones, smothered them with kisses and poured out thanksgivings.

Tom Sawyer the Pirate felt that this was the proudest moment of his life.

Chapter 18

That was Tom's great secret—the scheme to return home with his brother pirates and attend their own funerals. They had paddled over to the Missouri shore on a log, and had then crept through back lanes and alleys and finished their sleep in the gallery of the church among a chaos of invalided benches.

At breakfast, Monday morning, Aunt Polly and Mary were very loving to Tom, and very attentive to his wants. Aunt Polly said:

"Well, Tom, you could have come over and given me a hint some way that you warn't dead, but only run off." Then Tom told Polly a lie about his certain dream. He cunningly related everything he had seen and heard secretly that night. Aunt Polly was surprised that Tom had such a long dream which all came out true.

As the children left for school, the old lady went to call on Mrs. Harper and vanquish her realism with Tom's marvellous dream.

What a hero Tom was become, now!

At school the children made so much of him and of Joe. And finally, when they got out their pipes and went serenely puffing around, the very summit of glory was reached.

Tom decided that he could be independent of Becky Thatcher now. Glory was sufficient. Now that he was distinguished, maybe she would be wanting to "make up." Presently she arrived. Tom pretended not to see her. He moved away and joined a group of boys and girls and began to talk. But she continued observing him. Presently she gave over skylarking, and moved irresolutely about, sighing once or twice and glancing furtively and wistfully toward Tom. Then she observed that now Tom was talking more particularly to Amy Lawrence than to any one else. She felt a sharp pang and grew disturbed and uneasy at once; and tried to go away.

Becky started talking to a girl Mary Austin within hearing distance of Tom. She told her about the picnic, inviting all the girls and boys "that's friends to me—or wants to be"; and she glanced ever so furtively at Tom, but he talked right along to Amy Lawrence about the terrible storm on the island.

And so on, with clapping of joyful hands till all the group had begged for invitations but Tom and Amy. Then Tom turned coolly away, still talking, and took Amy with him. Becky's lips trembled and the tears came to her eyes. Then she roused up, with a vindictive cast in her eye, and said she knew what SHE'D do.

At recess Tom continued his flirtation with Amy. And he kept drifting about to find Becky and lacerate her with the performance. At last he spied her, but there was a sudden falling of his mercury. She was sitting cosily on a little bench behind the schoolhouse looking at a picture-book with Alfred Temple—and so absorbed were they, and their heads so close together over the book, that they did not seem to be conscious of anything in the world besides. Jealousy ran red-hot through Tom's veins. He began to hate himself for throwing away the chance Becky had offered for a reconciliation. He even called himself a fool. Amy chatted happily along, as they walked,

Amy chatted happily along, as they walked.

but Tom's tongue had lost its function. He did not hear what Amy was saying.

Amy's happy prattle became intolerable. Tom wanted to get rid of her somehow. He said he had to do many important things.

Tom fled home at noon. His conscience could not endure any more of Amy's grateful happiness, and his jealousy could bear no more of the other distress. Becky resumed her picture inspections with Alfred, but as the minutes dragged along and no Tom came to suffer, her triumph began to cloud and she lost interest; gravity and absent-mindedness followed, and then melancholy.

At last she grew entirely miserable. Alfred tried to soothe her but to no avail. At last she said: "Go away and leave me alone, can't you! I hate you!"

So the boy halted, wondering what he could have done. He was humiliated and angry. He easily guessed his way to the truth—the girl had simply made a convenience of him to vent her spite upon Tom Sawyer. He wished there was some way to get that boy into trouble without much risk to himself. Tom's spelling-book fell under his eye. Here was his opportunity. He gratefully opened to the lesson for the afternoon and poured ink upon the page.

Becky saw this and wanted to tell Tom about it, but then she changed her mind in view of Tom's treatment of her. She resolved to let him get shipped on the damaged spelling book's account, and to hate him forever, into the bargain.

Chapter 19

Aunt was awfully angry with Tom. She said, "Here I go over to Sereny Harper, expecting I'm going to make her believe about that dream, when lo and behold you she'd found out from Joe that you was over here and heard all the talk we had that night."

Tom felt very small and mean and said, "Auntie, I wish I hadn't done it—but I didn't think."

"Oh, child, you never think. You never think of anything but your own selfishness. You could think to come all the way over here from Jackson's Island in the night to laugh at our troubles, and you could think to fool me with a lie about a dream; but you couldn't ever think to pity us and save us from sorrow."

"Auntie, I know now it was mean, I didn't come over here to laugh at you that night."

"What did you come for, then?"

"It was to tell you not to be uneasy about us, because we hadn't got drownded."

Aunt was, however, not ready to believe it.

Then Tom said, "Why, you see, when you got to talking about the funeral, I just got all full of the idea of our coming and hiding in the church, and I couldn't somehow bear to spoil it. So I just put the bark back in my pocket and kept mum."

"What bark?"

"The bark I had wrote on to tell you we'd gone pirating. I wish, now, you'd waked up when I kissed you—I do, honest."

At this, the hard lines in his aunt's face relaxed and a sudden tenderness dawned in her eyes.

She said: "Kiss me again, Tom!—and be off with you to school, now."

The moment he was gone, she ran to a closet and got out the ruin of a jacket which Tom had gone pirating in.

She sought the jacket pocket. A moment later she was reading Tom's piece of bark through flowing tears and saying: "I could forgive the boy, now, if he'd committed a million sins!"

Chapter 20

There was something about Aunt Polly's manner, when she kissed Tom, that swept away his low spirits and made him lighthearted and happy again. He started to school and had the luck of coming upon Becky Thatcher at the head of Meadow Lane. He went to the girl asking her to make up.

The girl stopped and said:

"I'll thank you to keep yourself TO yourself, Mr. Thomas Sawyer. I'll never speak to you again." She tossed her head and passed on.

Mr. Dobbins the village school master had a mysterious book in his drawer. Now, as Becky was passing by the desk, she noticed that the key was in the lock! She found herself alone, and the next instant she had the book in her hands. The title-page—Professor Somebody's ANATOMY—carried no information

She had the book in her hands.

to her mind; so she began to turn the leaves. She came at once upon a handsomely engraved and colored frontispiece—a human figure, stark naked.

At that moment a shadow fell on the page and Tom Sawyer stepped in at the door and caught a glimpse of the picture. Becky snatched at the book to close it, and had the hard luck to tear the pictured page half down the middle. She thrust the volume into the desk, turned the key, and burst out crying with shame and vexation.

There was an exchange of angry words between the two childern. However, Tom decided not to tell Mr. Dobbins. He'll know of it himself on reading her face.

The master came and presently the spelling-book discovery was made.

Tom took his whipping and went back to his seat not at all broken-hearted.

A whole hour drifted by, the master sat nodding in his throne. By and by, Mr. Dobbins straightened himself up, yawned, then unlocked his desk, and reached for his book. Mr. Dobbins then took his book and settled himself in his chair to read!

Tom shot a glance at Becky. He had seen a hunted and helpless rabbit look as she did. Instantly he forgot his quarrel with her. Quick—something must be done! Good!—he had an inspiration! He would run and snatch the book, spring through the door and fly. But his resolution shook for one little instant, and the chance was lost—the master opened the volume. Too late. Then he spoke: "Who tore this book?"

There was not a sound. One could have heard a pin drop. The master searched face after face for signs of guilt.

A thought shot like lightning through Tom's brain and he shouted—"I done it!"

The school stared in perplexity at this incredible folly. When Tom stepped forward to go to his punishment the surprise, the gratitude, the adoration that shone upon him out of poor Becky's eyes seemed pay enough for a hundred floggings. Inspired by the splendor of his own act, he took without an outcry the most merciless flaying that even Mr. Dobbins had ever administered.

Tom went to bed that night planning vengeance against Alfred Temple; for with shame and repentance Becky had told him all, not forgetting her own treachery; but even the longing for vengeance had to give way, soon, to pleasanter musings, and he fell asleep at last with Becky's latest words lingering dreamily in his ear—

"Tom, how COULD you be so noble!"

Chapter 21

Vacation was approaching. The schoolmaster, always severe, grew severer and more exacting than ever, for he wanted the school to make a good showing on "Examination" day. He was particularly cruel to small childern, and they were always plotting against him. At last they conspired together and hit upon a plan that promised a dazzling victory. They swore in the sign-painter's boy, told him the scheme, and asked his help. He had his own reasons for being delighted, for the master boarded in his father's family and had given the boy ample cause to hate him.

In the fulness of time the interesting occasion arrived. At eight in the evening the schoolhouse was brilliantly lighted, and adorned with wreaths and festoons of foliage and flowers. The master sat throned in his great chair upon a raised platform, with his black-

Tom retired, utterly defeated.

board behind him. There were seperate rows for dignitaries of the town, parents of the pupils, citizens and scholar participants. All were well-dressed and were in high spirits. First a little boy and then a little girl presented their items.

Then Tom Sawyer stepped forward with "Give me liberty or give me death" speech, and broke down in the middle of it. Tom struggled awhile and then retired, utterly defeated.

Then several other declamatory items were presented by the young ladies. A prevalent feature in these compositions was a nursed and petted melancholy; another was a wasteful and opulent gush of "fine language"; another was a tendency to lug in by the ears particularly prized words and phrases until they were worn entirely out.

Let us return to the "Examination." The first composition that was read was one entitled "Is this, then, Life?"

Then arose a slim, melancholy girl, and read a "poem."

A MISSOURI MAIDEN'S FAREWELL TO ALABAMA

Next appeared a dark-complexioned, black-eyed, black-haired young lady, who began to read in a measured, solemn tone:

"A VISION"

This composition was considered to be the very finest effort of the evening.

Now the master, turned his back to the audience, and began to draw a map of America on the blackboard. But he made a sad business of it with his unsteady hand, and a smothered titter rippled over the house.

He threw his entire attention upon his work, now, as if determined not to be put down by the mirth. He felt that all eyes were fastened upon him; he imagined he was succeeding, and yet the tittering continued; it even manifestly increased. And well it might. There was a garret above, pierced with a scuttle over his head; and down through this scuttle came a cat, suspended around the haunches by a string; she had a rag tied about her head and jaws to keep her from mewing; as she slowly descended she curved upward and clawed at the string, she swung downward and clawed at the intangible air.

The tittering rose higher and higher—the cat was within six inches of the absorbed teacher's head—down, down, a little lower, and she grabbed his wig with her desperate claws, clung to it, and was snatched up into the garret in an instant with her trophy still in her possession! And how the light did blaze abroad from the master's bald pate—for the sign-painter's boy had GILDED it!

That broke up the meeting. The boys were avenged. Vacation had come.

Chapter 22

Tom joined the new order of Cadets of Temperance, being attracted by the showy character of their "regalia." He promised to abstain from smoking, chewing, and profanity as long as he remained a member. But Tom soon found himself tormented with a desire to drink and swear. He fixed his hopes upon old Judge Frazer, justice of the peace, who was apparently on his deathbed.

But the Judge had a most discouraging way of fluctuating. Tom was disgusted; He handed in his resignation at once—and that night the Judge suffered a relapse and died. Tom resolved that he would never trust a man like that again.

The funeral was a fine thing. The Cadets paraded in a style calculated to kill the late member with envy.

As Tom crept to bed, there came that night a terrific storm.

Tom was a free boy again. He could drink and swear, now—but found to his surprise that he did not want to. The simple fact that he could, took the desire away, and the charm of it.

Then came the measles.

During two long weeks Tom lay a prisoner, dead to the world and its happenings. When he got upon his feet at last, a melancholy change had come over everything and every creature. There had been a "revival," and everybody had "got religion," not only the adults, but even the boys and girls.

Tom went about, hoping against hope for the sight of one blessed sinful face, but disappointment crossed him everywhere. He found boys Joe Harper boys Ben Rogers, Jim Hollis, Huckleberry Finn all occupied in one or other religious activity. His heart broke and he crept home and to bed realizing that he alone of all the town was lost, forever and forever.

And that night there came on a terrific storm, with driving rain, awful claps of thunder and blinding sheets of lightning. He believed he had taxed the forbearance of the powers above to the extremity of endurance and that this was the result.

By and by the tempest spent itself and died without accomplishing its object.

The next day the doctors were back; Tom had relapsed. The three weeks he spent on his back this time seemed an entire age.

Chapter 23

At last the sleepy atmosphere was stirred and vigorously: the murder trial came on in the court. It became the absorbing topic of village talk immediately. Tom could not get away from it. Every reference to the murder sent a shudder to his heart. He took Huck to a lonely place to have a talk with him.

Tom was satisfied after talking to Huck that he had not revealed the fact of murder in their presence to anybody.

So they swore again with dread solemnities.

"What is the talk around, Huck?

"Talk? Well, it's just Muff Potter, Muff Potter, Muff Potter all the time.

Don't you feel sorry for him, sometimes?"

"Most always—most always. I wish we could get him out of there."

The boys had a long talk, but it brought them little comfort.

The boys did as they had often done before—went to the cell grating and gave Potter some tobacco and matches. There were no guards.

His gratitude for their gifts had always smote their consciences before—it cut deeper this time. They felt cowardly and treacherous to the last degree when Potter said:

"You've been mighty good to me, boys—better'n anybody else in this town. And I don't forget it, I don't. Often I says to myself, says I, 'I used to mend all the boys' kites and things, and show 'em where the good fishin' places was, and befriend 'em what I could, and now they've all forgot old Muff when he's in trouble; but Tom don't, and Huck don't—THEY don't forget him, says I, 'and I don't forget them.'"

Tom went home miserable, and his dreams that night were full of horrors. The next day and the day after, he hung about the courtroom, drawn by an almost irresistible impulse to go in, but forcing himself to stay out. Huck was having the same experience. At the end of the second day the village talk was to the effect that Injun Joe's evidence stood firm and unshaken, and that there was not the slightest question as to what the jury's verdict would be.

Tom was out late, that night, and came to bed through the window. He was in a tremendous state of excitement. It was hours before he got to sleep. All the village flocked to the court-house the next morning, for this was to be the great day.

After a long wait the jury filed in and took their places; shortly afterward, Potter, pale and haggard, timid and hopeless, was brought in, with chains upon him, and seated where all the curious eyes could stare at him; no less conspicuous was Injun Joe, stolid as ever. There was another pause, and then the judge arrived and the sheriff proclaimed the opening of the court.

Now a witness was called who testified that he found Muff Potter washing in the brook, at an early hour of the morning that the murder was discovered, and that he immediately sneaked away.

The next witness proved the finding of the knife near the corpse.

With the deposition of Tom the whole situation changed.

A third witness swore he had often seen the knife in Potter's possession.

Counsel for Potter declined to question any of the witnesses.

Counsel for the prosecution now said:

"By the oaths of citizens, we have fastened this awful crime, beyond all possibility of question, upon the unhappy prisoner at the bar. We rest our case here."

Then Counsel for the defence rose and said:

"Your honor, in our remarks at the opening of this trial, we foreshadowed our purpose to prove that our client did this fearful deed while under the influence of a blind and irresponsible delirium produced by drink. We shall not offer that plea." [Then to the clerk:] "Call Thomas Sawyer!"

With the deposition of Tom, the whole situation changed.

Tom began—hesitatingly at first, but as he warmed to his subject his words flowed more and more easily; every eye fixed itself upon him. The strain upon pent emotion reached its climax when the boy said:

"—and as the doctor fetched the board around and Muff Potter fell, Injun Joe jumped with the knife and—"

Crash! Quick as lightning the half-breed sprang for a window, tore his way through all opposers, and was gone!

Chapter 24

Tom was a glittering hero once more. His days were days of splendor and exultation to him, but his nights were seasons of horror. Injun Joe infested all his dreams, and always with doom in his eye. Poor Huck was in the same state of wretchedness and terror, for Tom had told the whole story to the lawyer the night before the great day of the trial, and Huck was sore afraid that his share in the business might leak out.

Half the time Tom was afraid Injun Joe would never be captured; the other half he was afraid he would be. He felt sure he never could draw a safe breath again until that man was dead and he had seen the corpse.

Rewards had been offered, the country had been scoured, but no Injun Joe was found, and Tom felt just as insecure as he was before.

Chapter 25

There comes a time in every rightly-constructed boy's life when he has a raging desire to go somewhere and dig for hidden treasure. This desire suddenly came upon Tom one day. He sallied out to find Huck who would answer. Tom took him to a private place and opened the matter to him confidentially. Huck was willing. "Where'll we dig?" said Huck.

It's hid in mighty particular places, Huck —sometimes on islands, sometimes in rotten chests under the end of a limb of an old dead tree, just where the shadow falls at midnight; but mostly under the floor in ha'nted houses."

"Who hides it?"

"Why, robbers, of course."

"Don't they come after it any more?"

"No, they think they will, but they generally forget the marks, or else they die. Anyway, it lays there a long time and gets rusty; and by and by somebody finds an old yellow paper that tells how to find the marks—a paper that's got to be ciphered over about a week because it's mostly signs and hy'roglyphics."

The boys had long talk about possible places for treasure, about kings, diamonds, witches, ghosts, etc.

Then Tom said, "Let's tackle that old deadlimb tree on the hill t'other side of Still-House branch?"

"I'm agreed."

So they got a crippled pick and a shovel, and set out on their three-mile tramp. They arrived hot and panting.

They worked and sweated for half an hour. No result. They toiled another half-hour. Still no result.

So they chose a new spot and began again. The labor dragged a little, but still they made no progress.

They tried some other places, but without any result.

Then Tom said, "Sometimes witches interfere. I reckon maybe that's what's the trouble now."

Tom and Huck hunting for treasure.

"Shucks! Witches ain't got no power in the daytime."

"Well, that's so. I didn't think of that. What a blamed lot of fools we are! You got to find out where the shadow of the limb falls at midnight, and that's where you dig!"

"We've fooled away all this work for nothing. Now hang it all, we got to come back in the night. It's an awful long way. Can you get out?"

"I bet I will. We've got to do it to-night, too, because if somebody sees these holes they'll know in a minute what's here and they'll go for it."

"Well, I'll come around and maow to-night."

"All right. Let's hide the tools in the bushes."

The boys were there that night, about the appointed time. They sat in the shadow waiting. It was a lonely place. They marked where the shadow fell, and began to dig. Their hopes commenced to rise. The hole deepened and still deepened, but every time their hearts jumped to hear the pick strike upon something, they only suffered a new disappointment. It was only a stone or a chunk.

Then Tom suggested that they should try their luck at a haunted house.

So, they decided to take chances at a haunted house at some stage, and took their way homeward through the woods.

Chapter 26

About noon the next day the boys arrived at the dead tree; they had come for their tools. Tom was impatient to go to the haunted house; Huck was measurably so, also—but suddenly the latter remembered that it was Friday that day, which was not a lucky day for such things.

On Saturday, shortly after noon, the boys were at the dead tree again. As their second attempt here also failed, they took their tools and reached the haunted house and were about to go down and begin work when—Tom heard some sound.

The boys stretched themselves upon the floor with their eyes to knot-holes in the planking, and lay waiting in fear.

Two men entered. Each boy said to himself: "There's the old deaf and dumb Spaniard that's been about town once or twice lately—never saw t'other man before."

"T'other" was a ragged, unkempt creature, with nothing very pleasant in his face. They sat down on the ground, facing the door, with their backs to the wall, and the speaker continued his remarks.

The boys soon recognized from his voice that the other man was Injun Joe. The two had a luncheon there. Then Joe said to the Spaniard:

"I'm dead for sleep! It's your turn to watch."

He curled down in the weeds and soon began to snore. His comrade stirred him once or twice and he became quiet. Presently the watcher began to nod; his head drooped lower and lower, both men began to snore now.

Now, as the sun was setting, one snore ceased. Injun Joe sat up,—stirred the other up, and said, "Nearly time for us to be moving, pard. What'll we do with what little swag we've got left?"

"I don't know—leave it here as we've always done, I reckon. No use to take it away till we start south. Six hundred and fifty in silver's something to carry."

They kept about fifity dollars for themselves and buried the remaining six hundred dollars in a corner.

The boys forgot all their fears, all their miseries in an instant. With gloating eyes they watched every movement. Now, there would not be any bothersome uncertainty as to where to dig.

Meanwhile, Joe's knife struck upon something. It was a half-rotten box.

"Man, it's money!"

It contained thousands of dollars left by Murrel's gang.

"Now you won't need to do that job," said the comrade.

The half-breed frowned. Said he:

"You don't know all about that thing. 'Tain't robbery altogether—it's REVENGE!". "I'll need your help in it. When it's finished—then Texas. Go home to your Nance and your kids, and stand by till you hear from me."

"Well—if you say so; what'll we do with this—bury it again?"

"We'll take it to my den—Number Two—under the cross."

"Yes. [Ravishing delight overhead.] NO! by the great Sachem, no! [Profound distress overhead.] I'd nearly forgot. That pick had fresh earth on it! [The boys were sick with terror in a moment.] What business has a pick and a shovel here? What business with fresh earth on them? Who brought them here—and where are they gone? Have you heard anybody?—seen anybody? What! bury it again and leave them to come and see the ground disturbed? Not exactly—not exactly. We'll take it to my den."

"Why, of course! Might have thought of that before. You mean Number One?"

"No—Number Two—under the cross. The other place is bad—too common."

"All right. It's nearly dark enough to start."

Injun Joe got up and went about from window to window cautiously peeping out. Presently he said:

"Who could have brought those tools here? Do you reckon they can be up-stairs?"

The boys' breath forsook them. Injun Joe put his hand on his knife, halted a moment, undecided, and then turned toward the stairway. The boys thought of the closet, but their strength was gone. The steps came creaking up the stairs. Immediately, there was a crash of rotten timbers and Injun Joe landed on the ground amid the debris of the ruined stairway. He gathered himself up cursing, and his comrade said:

"Now what's the use of all that? If it's anybody, and they're up there, let them STAY there—who cares? In my opinion, whoever hove those things in here caught a sight of us and took us for ghosts or devils or something. I'll bet they're running yet."

Joe grumbled awhile; then he agreed with his friend. Shortly afterward they slipped out of the house in the deepening twilight, and moved toward the river with their precious box.

Tom and Huck resolved to keep a lookout for that Spaniard when he should come to town spying out for chances to do his revengeful job, and follow him to "Number Two," wherever that might be. Then a ghastly thought occurred to Tom.

"Revenge? What if he means US, Huck!"

"Oh, don't!" said Huck, nearly fainting.

They talked it all over, and as they entered town they agreed to believe that he might possibly mean nobody but Tom, since only Tom had testified.

Chapter 27

The adventure of the day mightily tormented Tom's dreams that night. Even during the day he was haunted by reveries of unimaginable "hundreds" and "thousands" of dollars.

He would snatch a hurried breakfast and go and find Huck. Huck was sitting on the gunwale of a flatboat looking very melancholy.

The boys wanted to track down the puzzling Number Two. At first they thought it might be number of a house. Then, they thought it might be the number of a room in a tavern. There were only two taverns in the town. So, they decided to find it out.

So Tom said, "You stay here, Huck, till I come."

Tom was off at once. He found that in the best tavern No 2 had long been occupied by a lawyer. In the less ostentatious house, No. 2 was a mystery. The tavern-keeper's young son said it was kept locked all the time, and he never saw anybody go into it or come out of it except at night.

He told Huck about it. Then he said:

"I'll tell you. The back door of that No. 2 is the door that comes out into that little close alley between the tavern and the old rattle trap of a brick store. Now you get hold of all the door-keys you can find, and I'll nip all of auntie's, and the first dark night we'll go there and try 'em. And mind you, keep a lookout for Injun Joe, because he said he was going to drop into town and spy around once more for a chance to get his revenge. If you see him, you just follow him; and if he don't go to that No. 2, that ain't the place."

"Lordy, I don't want to foller him by myself!"

However, Tom said, "You bet I'll follow him, if it's dark, Huck. Why, he might 'a' found out he couldn't get his revenge, and be going right after that money."

"It's so, Tom, it's so. I'll foller him; I will, by jingoes!"

"Now you're TALKING! Don't you every weaken, Huck, and I won't."

Chapter 28

That night Tom and Huck were ready for their adventure. They hung about the neighborhood of the tavern until after nine, one watching the alley at a distance and the other the tavern door. Nobody entered the alley or left it; nobody resembling the Spaniard entered or left the tavern door.

Tuesday the boys had the same ill luck. Also Wednesday. But Thursday night promised better. Tom slipped out in good season with his aunt's old tin lantern, and a large towel to blindfold it with. He hid the lantern in Huck's sugar hogshead and the watch began. An hour before midnight the tavern closed up and its lights (the only ones thereabouts) were put out. No Spaniard had been seen. Nobody had entered or left the alley.

Tom got his lantern, lit it in the hogshead, wrapped it closely in the towel, and the two

Tom lit the lantern in the hogshead and wrapped it in the towel and slipped out.

adventurers crept in the gloom toward the tavern. Huck stood sentry and Tom felt his way into the alley.

Then there was a season of waiting anxiety that weighed upon Huck's spirits like a mountain. It seemed hours since Tom had disappeared. Suddenly there was a flash of light and Tom came tearing by him: "Run!" said he; "run, for your life!"

The boys never stopped till they reached the shed of a deserted slaughter-house at the lower end of the village. As soon as Tom got his breath he said:

"Huck, it was awful! Well, without noticing what I was doing, I took hold of the knob, and open comes the door! It warn't locked! I hoped in, and shook off the towel, and, GREAT CAESAR'S GHOST!"

"What!—what'd you see, Tom?"

"Huck, I most stepped onto Injun Joe's hand! He was lying there, sound asleep on the floor, with his old patch on his eye and his arms spread out.

Drunk, I reckon. I just grabbed that towel and started!"

"Say, Tom, did you see that box?"

"Huck, I didn't wait to look around. I didn't see the box, I didn't see the cross. I didn't see anything but a bottle and a tin cup on the floor by Injun Joe; yes, I saw two barrels and lots more bottles in the room.

But say, Tom, now's a mighty good time to get that box, if Injun Joe's drunk."

"Lookyhere, Huck, less not try that thing any more till we know Injun Joe's not in there. It's too scary. Now, if we watch every night, we'll be dead sure to see him go out, some time or other, and then we'll snatch that box quicker'n lightning."

"Well, I'm agreed. I'll watch the whole night long, and I'll do it every night, too, if you'll do the other part of the job."

"Now, Huck, the storm's over, and I'll go home. It'll begin to be daylight in a couple of hours. You go back and watch that long, will you?"

"I said I would, Tom, and I will. I'll ha'nt that tavern every night for a year! I'll sleep all day and I'll stand watch all night."

"That's all right. Now, where you going to sleep?"

"In Ben Rogers' hayloft. He lets me, and so does his pap's nigger man, Uncle Jake. That's a mighty good nigger, Tom. He likes me, becuz I don't every act as if I was above him.

Chapter 29

The first thing Tom heard on Friday morning was a glad piece of news —Judge Thatcher's family had come back to town the night before. Becky took the chief place in the boy's interest. He saw her and they had an exhausting good time playing "hi-spy" and "gully-keeper" with a crowd of their schoolmates. Becky teased her mother to appoint the next day for the long-promised and long-delayed picnic, and she consented.

The invitations were sent out before sunset.

Morning came, eventually, and by ten or eleven o'clock a giddy and rollicking company were gathered at Judge Thatcher's, and everything was ready for a start. It was not the custom for elderly people to mar the picnics with their presence. The old steam ferryboat was chartered for the occasion.

Three miles below town the ferryboat stopped at the mouth of a woody hollow and tied up. The crowd swarmed ashore and soon the forest distances and craggy heights echoed far and near with shoutings and laughter. By-and-by somebody shouted:

"Who's ready for the cave?"

Everybody was. Bundles of candles were procured, and straightway there was a general scamper up the hill.

Every few steps other lofty and still narrower crevices branched from it on either hand—for McDougal's cave was but a vast labyrinth of crooked aisles that ran into each other and out again and led nowhere.

By—and—by, one group after another came straggling back to the mouth of the cave, panting, hilarious, and entirely delighted with the success of the day. Then they were astonished to find that they had been taking no note of time and that night was about at hand. When the ferryboat with her wild freight pushed into the stream, nobody cared sixpence for the wasted time but the captain of the craft.

Huck secretly following the two men.

Huck was already upon his watch when the ferryboat's lights went glinting past the wharf. He heard no noise on board. He wondered what boat it was, and why she did not stop at the wharf, and then he dropped her out of his mind and put his attention upon his business.

It was after eleven o'clock that a noise fell upon his ear. He was all attention in an instant. The alley door closed softly. He sprang to the corner of the brick store. The next moment two men brushed by him, and one seemed to have something under his arm. It must be that box! So they were going to remove the treasure. Huck stepped out and glided along behind the men, cat-like, with bare feet, allowing them to keep just far enough ahead not to be invisible.

They moved up the river street three blocks, then turned to the left up a cross-street. They went straight ahead, then, until they came to the path that led up Cardiff Hill; They passed on, up the summit. They plunged into the narrow path between the tall sumach bushes, and were at once hidden in the gloom. Huck closed up and shortened his distance, now, for they would never be able to see him.

Heavens, was everything lost! He knew where he was. He knew he was within five steps of the stile leading into Widow Douglas' grounds. Very well, he thought, let them bury it there; it won't be hard to find.

Now there was a voice—a very low voice—Injun Joe's:

"Damn her, maybe she's got company—there's lights, late as it is."

"I can't see any."

This was that stranger's voice—the stranger of the haunted house. A deadly chill went to Huck's heart—this, then, was the "revenge" job! His thought was, to fly. Then he remembered that the Widow Douglas had been kind to him more than once, and maybe these men were going to murder her.

Then he heard Injun Joe's voice:

"I tell you again, as I've told you before, I don't care for her swag—you may have it. But her husband was rough on me—many times horsewhipped in front of the jail, like a nigger!—with all the town looking on!

"Oh, don't kill her! Don't do that!"

"Kill? Who said anything about killing? When you want to get revenge on a woman you don't kill her—bosh! you go for her looks. You slit her nostrils—you notch her ears like a sow! I'll tie her to the bed. If she bleeds to death, is that my fault? My friend, you'll help me in this thing— If you flinch, I'll kill you.

"Well, if it's got to be done, let's get at it. The quicker the better."

"No—we'll wait till the lights are out—there's no hurry."

Huck held his breath and stepped gingerly back. He stepped quickly but cautiously along. Down, down he sped, till he reached the Welshman's. He banged at the door, and presently the heads of the old man and his two stalwart sons were thrust from windows.

As Huck was let in, he said, "Please don't ever tell I told you." "Please don't—I'd be killed, sure.

"By George, he HAS got something to tell. Exclaimed the old man; "out with it and nobody here'll ever tell, lad."

Three minutes later the old man and his sons, well armed, were up the hill. There was a lagging, anxious silence, and then all of a sudden there was an explosion of firearms and a cry.

Huck sprang away and sped down the hill as fast as his legs could carry him.

Chapter 30

As the dawn appeared on Sunday, Huck came groping up the hill and rapped gently at the old Welshman's door. The old man explained how the rascals escaped even when they were within firing range.

The man further said, "As soon as it is light the sheriff and a gang are going to beat up the woods. My boys will be with them presently. I wish we had some sort of description of those rascals—'twould help a good deal."

Then Huck said, "One's the old deaf and dumb Spaniard that's ben around here once or twice, and t'other's a mean-looking, ragged‑"

The old man at once sent his boys to go and tell the Sheriff. As they were leaving the room Huck sprang up and exclaimed:

"Oh, please don't tell ANYbody it was me that blowed on them! Oh, please!"

The old man promised secrecy and asked several questions.

At first, Huck tried to hide Injun Joe's identity, but later disclosed it, on old man's renewed promise of secrecy and protection.

Then the old man said that before going to bed, they had got a lantern and examined the stile and its vicinity for marks of blood. They found none, but captured a bulky bundle of burglar's tools.

Huck got a sort of satisfaction that the bundle did not contain the treasure which must be still in No. 2, the men would be captured and jailed that day, and he and Tom could seize the gold that night without any trouble or any fear of interruption.

Just as breakfast was completed there was a knock at the door. Huck jumped for a hiding-place, for he had no mind to be connected even remotely with the late event. The Welshman admitted several ladies and gentlemen, among them the Widow Douglas, and noticed that groups of citizens were climbing up the hill—to stare at the stile. So the news had spread. The Welshman had to tell the story of the night to the visitors. The widow's gratitude for her preservation was outspoken.

The old man asked Huck to tell him everything about the Spaniard and Injun Joe.

There was no Sabbath-school during day-school vacation, but everybody was early at church. When the sermon was finished, Judge Thatcher's wife dropped alongside of Mrs. Harper as she moved down the aisle with the crowd and said:

"Is my Becky going to sleep all day? I just expected she would be tired to death."

"Your Becky?"

"Yes," with a startled look—"didn't she stay with you last night?"

"Why, no."

Mrs. Thatcher turned pale, and sank into a pew, just as Aunt Polly, talking briskly with a friend, passed by. Aunt Polly said:

"Good-morning, Mrs. Thatcher. Good-morning, Mrs. Harper. I've got a boy that's turned up missing. I reckon my Tom stayed at your house last night—one of you."

Mrs. Thatcher shook her head feebly and turned paler than ever.

"He didn't stay with us," said Mrs. Harper, beginning to look uneasy. A marked anxiety came into Aunt Polly's face.

Whispers passed along, and a boding uneasiness took possession of every countenance. One young man finally blurted out his fear that they were still in the cave! Mrs. Thatcher swooned away. Aunt Polly fell to crying and wringing her hands.

The alarm swept from lip to lip, from group to group, from street to street, and within five minutes the bells were wildly clanging and the whole town was up! The Cardiff Hill episode sank into instant insignificance, the burglars were forgotten, horses were saddled, skiffs were manned, the ferryboat ordered out, and before the horror was half an hour old, two hundred men were pouring down highroad and river toward the cave.

All the news that could be gained was that remotenesses of the cavern were being ransacked that had never been visited before. In one place, far from the section usually traversed by tourists, the names "BECKY & TOM" had been found traced upon the rocky wall with candle-smoke, and near at hand a grease-soiled bit of ribbon. Mrs. Thatcher recognized the ribbon and cried over it.

Three dreadful days and nights dragged their tedious hours along, and the village sank into a hopeless stupor. No one had heart for anything. The accidental discovery, just made, that the proprietor of the Temperance Tavern kept liquor on his premises, scarcely fluttered the public pulse.

However, as Huck learnt that nothing but liquor had been found, he thought the treasure was gone forever. These thoughts worked their dim way through Huck's mind, and under the weariness they gave him he fell asleep. The widow continued taking care of Huck who was in delirium due to fever and wearniess. ▢▢▢

Chapter 31

Now to return to Tom and Becky's share in the picnic. They tripped along the murky aisles with the rest of the company, visiting the familiar wonders of the cave. They had got separated from the rest of picnikers without noticing it. Then, they felt they were trapped in the labyrinthine caves. They tried hard but could not find a way out. All they could do was to move, keep moving—aimlessly.

At last Becky's frail limbs refused to carry her farther. Fatigue bore so heavily upon her that she drowsed off to sleep. Tom was sat looking into her drawn face by-and-by a smile dawned and rested there.

Then Becky broke the silence:

"Tom, I am so hungry!"

Tom took something out of his pocket. It was a piece of cake which he had saved from

Tom and Becky in the cave.

picnic to dream on their wedding as wedding cake.

Tom divided the cake and Becky ate with good appetite, while Tom nibbled at his moiety.

Suddenly they heard a sound like the faintest, far-off shout. Instantly Tom answered it, and leading Becky by the hand, started groping down the corridor in its direction.

Presently he listened again; again the sound was heard, and apparently a little nearer.

"It's them!" said Tom; "they're coming! Come along, Becky—we're all right now!"

The joy of the prisoners was almost overwhelming. However soon the sounds fainted and had gone altogether.

They had to sleep there. When they awoke an idea struck Tom. He made an effort with the help of the kite line kept in his packet, and at that moment, not twenty yards away, a human hand, holding a candle, appeared from behind a rock! Tom lifted up a glorious shout, and instantly that hand was followed by the body it belonged to—Injun Joe's! Tom was paralyzed.

He was vastly gratified the next moment, to see the "Spaniard" take to his heels and get himself out of sight without harming him.

Becky was very weak and unable to move. She told Tom to go with the kite line and explore. Tom kissed Becky, with a choking sensation in his throat, and made a show of being confident of finding the searchers or an escape from the cave.

Chapter 32

Tuesday afternoon came, and waned to the twilight. The village of St. Petersburg still mourned. The lost children had not been found. Public prayers had been offered up for them. But still no good news came from the cave. The majority of the searchers had given up the quest and gone back to their daily avocations, saying that it was plain the children could never be found.

Mrs. Thatcher was very ill, and a great part of the time delirious. Aunt Polly had drooped into a settled melancholy, and her gray hair had grown almost white.

Away in the middle of the night a wild peal burst from the village bells, and in a moment the streets were swarming with frantic half-clad people, who shouted, "Turn out! turn out! they're found! they're found!"

The population massed itself and moved toward the river, met the children coming in an open carriage drawn by shouting citizens, thronged around it.

The village was illuminated; Thatcher and Aunt Polly's happiness was beyond description.

At home Tom told the history of the wonderful adventure, and how he made use of the kite line to come out of the cave with Becky. He learned of the Cardiff Hill event; also that the "ragged man's" body had eventually been found in the river near the ferry-landing; he had been drowned while trying to escape, perhaps.

About a fortnight after Tom's rescue from the cave, he started off to visit Huck. Judge Thatcher's house was on Tom's way, and he stopped to see Becky. The Judge and some friends set Tom to talking, and the Judge said,

"Nobody will get lost in that cave any more because I had its big door sheathed with boiler iron two weeks ago, and triple-locked—and I've got the keys."

Tom turned as white as a sheet, and said after water was brought and thrown into his face, "Oh, Judge, Injun Joe's in the cave!"

Chapter 33

Within a few minutes the news about the cave had spread, and a dozen skiff-loads of men were on their way to McDougal's cave, and the ferryboat, well filled with passengers, soon followed. Tom Sawyer was in the skiff that bore Judge Thatcher.

When the cave door was unlocked, a sorrowful sight presented itself in the dim twilight of the place. Injun Joe lay stretched upon the ground, dead.

Injun Joe's bowie-knife lay close by, its blade broken in two. The great foundation-beam of the door had been chipped and hacked through, with tedious labor. The poor fellow had lived on bats and bits of candle left by tourists, but ultimately had starved to death.

Injun Joe was buried near the mouth of the cave; and people flocked there in boats and wagons to get satisfaction equal to his hanging.

The morning after the funeral Tom took Huck to a private place to have an important talk.

The startling thing that Tom told Huck was that Injun Joe's money was in the cave and not in No. 2.

Tom suggested that they should go to the cave immediately. He said, "It's about five mile into there the way anybody but me would go, Huck, but there's a mighty short cut that they don't anybody but me know about. Huck, I'll take you right to it in a skiff. I'll float the skiff down there, and I'll pull it back again all by myself. You needn't ever turn your hand over."

A trifle afternoon the boys borrowed a small skiff from a citizen who was absent, and got under way at once. They reached "Cave Hollow," and then a hole behind a thick clump of sumach bushes.

Now Tom declared "Here you are! Look at it, Huck; it's the snuggest hole in this country. You just keep mum about it. All along I've been wanting to be a robber, but I knew I'd got to have a thing like this, and where to run across it was the bother. We've got it now, and we'll keep it quiet, only we'll let Joe Harper and Ben Rogers in—because of course there's got to be a Gang, or else there wouldn't be any style about it. Tom Sawyer's Gang—it sounds splendid, don't it, Huck?"

"Well, it just does, Tom. And who'll we rob?"

"Oh, most anybody. Waylay people—that's mostly the way."

The boys entered the hole, Tom in the lead. They toiled their way to the farther end of the tunnel; then made their spliced kite strings fast and moved on.

They went on, and presently entered and followed Tom's other corridor. Tom whispered:

"Huck, Look as far around the corner as you can. There—on the big rock over yonder—done with candle-smoke."

"Tom, it's a CROSS!"

"NOW where's your Number Two? 'UNDER THE CROSS,' hey? Right yonder's where I saw Injun Joe poke up his candle, Huck!"

Tom went first, cutting rude steps in the clay hill as he descended. Huck followed. The lads searched and researched this place, but in vain. Then Tom said:

Tom shows Huck the cross on a big rock in the cave.

"He said UNDER the cross. Well, this comes nearest to being under the cross."

But after surveying the place thoroughly Tom said, "I bet you the money IS under the rock. I'm going to dig in the clay."

Tom's "real Barlow" was out at once, and he had not dug four inches before he struck wood. "Hey, Huck!—you hear that?"

Huck began to dig and scratch now. Some boards were soon uncovered and removed. They had concealed a natural chasm which led under the rock. Tom turned a short curve, by-and-by, and exclaimed:

"My goodness, Huck, lookyhere!"

It was the treasure-box, sure enough, occupying a snug little cavern, along with an empty powder-keg, a couple of guns in leather cases, two or three pairs of old moccasins, a leather belt, and some other rubbish well soaked with the water-drip.

They put the money into the bags they had brought with them which they took upto the cross rock.

"Now less fetch the guns and things," said Huck. "No, Huck—leave them there. They're just the tricks to have when we go to robbing."

They presently emerged into the clump of sumach bushes and found the coast clear. As the sun dipped toward the horizon they pushed out and got under way. Tom skimmed up the shore and landed shortly after dark.

"Now, Huck," said Tom, "we'll hide the money in the loft of the widow's woodshed, and I'll come up in the morning and we'll count it and divide, and then we'll hunt up a place out in the woods for it where it will be safe."

He disappeared, and presently returned with the wagon, put the two small sacks into it, threw some old rags on top of them, and started off, dragging his cargo behind him. When the boys reached the Welshman's house, they stopped to rest. Just as they were about to move on, the Welshman stepped out. He took them to widow Douglas.

The place was grandly lighted, and everybody that was of any consequence in the village was there. The widow received the boys heartily though they were covered with clay and candle-grease.

She took them to a bedchamber and said:

"Now wash and dress yourselves. Here are two new suits of clothes. Get into them. We'll wait—come down when you are slicked up enough."

Then she left.

Chapter 34

Some minutes later the widow's guests were at the supper-table. At the proper time Mr. Jones made his little speech, in which he thanked the widow for the honor she was doing himself and his sons.

He sprung his secret about Huck's share in the adventure in the finest dramatic manner he was master of.

The widow said she meant to give Huck a home under her roof and have him educated; and that when she could spare the money she would start him in business in a modest way. Tom's chance was come. He said:

"Huck don't need it. Huck's rich."

Nobody believed it. Then Tom ran out of doors, and came back struggling with the weight of his sacks. He poured the mass of yellow coin upon the table and said:

Tom poured the mass of yellow coin upon the table.

"There—what did I tell you? Half of it's Huck's and half of it's mine!"

The spectacle took the general breath away. All gazed, nobody spoke for a moment. Then Tom explained everything to them.

The money was counted. The sum amounted to a little over twelve thousand dollars. It was more than any one present had ever seen at one time before.

Chapter 35

Tom's and Huck's windfall made a mighty stir in the poor little village of St. Petersburg. Wherever Tom and Huck appeared they were courted, admired, stared at. The village paper published biographical sketches of the boys. The Widow Douglas put Huck's money out at six per cent., and Judge Thatcher did the same with Tom's at Aunt Polly's request. Each lad had an income, now, that was simply prodigious—a dollar for every week-day in the year and half of the Sundays.

Judge Thatcher had conceived a great opinion of Tom. He said that no commonplace boy would ever have got his daughter out of the cave. When Becky told her father, in strict confidence, how Tom had taken her whipping at school, the Judge was visibly moved.

Judge Thatcher hoped to see Tom a great lawyer or a great soldier some day.

Huck Finn's wealth and the fact that he was now under the Widow Douglas' protection introduced him into society. The widow's servants kept him clean and neat, combed and brushed. He had to eat with a knife and fork; he had to use napkin, cup, and plate; he had to learn his book, he had to go to church; he had to talk in a proper manner. Whithersoever he turned, the bars and shackles of civilization shut him in and bound him hand and foot.

He bravely bore his miseries three weeks, and then one day turned up missing. For forty-eight hours the widow hunted for him everywhere in great distress. Early the third morning Tom Sawyer wisely went poking among some old empty hogsheads down behind the abandoned slaughter-house, and in one of them he found the refugee. Huck had slept there; he had just breakfasted upon some stolen odds and ends of food, and was lying off, now, in comfort, with his pipe. He was unkempt, uncombed, and clad in rags.

Tom routed him out, told him the trouble he had been causing, and urged him to go home. Huck's face lost its tranquil content, and he said:

"Don't talk about it, Tom. I've tried it, and it don't work. The widder's good to me, and friendly; but I can't stand their ways."

Tom saw his opportunity—

"Lookyhere, Huck, being rich ain't going to keep me back from turning robber." But Huck, we can't let you into the gang if you ain't respectable, you know."

Huck's joy was quenched.

"Can't let me in, Tom, Didn't you let me go for a pirate?"

"Yes, but that's different. A robber is more high-toned than what a pirate is—as a general thing. In most countries they're awful high up in the nobility—dukes and such."

"Now, Tom, hain't you always ben friendly to me? You wouldn't shet me out, would you, Tom?"

Finally Huck said:

"Well, I'll go back to the widder for a month and tackle it and see if I can come to stand it, if you'll let me b'long to the gang, Tom."

"All right, Huck, it's a whiz! Come along, old chap, and I'll ask the widow to let up on you a little, Huck."

"Will you, Tom—now will you? That's good. When you going to start the gang and turn robbers?"

"Oh, right off. We'll get the boys together and have the initiation to-night, maybe."

"What's that?"

"It's to swear to stand by one another, and never tell the gang's secrets, even if you're chopped all to flinders, and kill anybody and all his family that hurts one of the gang," and all that swearing's got to be done at midnight, in the lonesomest, awfulest place you can find—a ha'nted house is the best, but they're all ripped up now."

"Well, midnight's good, anyway, Tom."

"Yes, so it is. And you've got to swear on a coffin, and sign it with blood."

"Now, that's something LIKE! Why, it's a million times bullier than pirating. I'll stick to the widder till I rot, Tom; and if I git to be a reg'lar ripper of a robber, and everybody talking 'bout it, I reckon she'll be proud she snaked me in out of the wet."

36
Conclusion

So endeth this chronicle. It being strictly a history of a BOY, it must stop here; the story could not go much further without becoming the history of a MAN. When one writes a novel about grown people, he knows exactly where to stop—that is, with a marriage; but when he writes of juveniles, he must stop where he best can.

Most of the characters that perform in this book still live, and are prosperous and happy. Some day it may seem worth while to take up the story of the younger ones again and see what sort of men and women they turned out to be; therefore it will be wisest not to reveal any of that part of their lives at present.

GLOSSARY
(word-meanings)

1. *Anxiously* = worriedly
2. *Melancholy* = sadness
3. *Entire* = full, complete
4. *Genuine* = real
5. *Perennial* = permanent
6. *Finally* = at last
7. *Enthusiasm* = zeal, earnestness
8. *Pirates* = sea-robbers
9. *Exhausted* = tired
10. *Revealed* = divulged, laid bare
11. *Quivering* = shaking, trembling
12. *Blissfully* = sadly
13. *Conspired* = plotted
14. *Manifestly* = openly, clearly
15. *Proclaimed* = announced, declared
16. *Timid* = cowardly
17. *Alley* = narrow street
18. *Procured* = got
19. *Blurted out* = spoke out loudly
20. *Gratified* = satisfied

Short Questions

1. What did Tom say to Aunt Polly when he smelt danger from her?
2. What were the length and height of the fence that Tom had to whitewash?
3. According to the author what is the difference between work and play?
4. What did Tom do with the flower that the little blue-eyed girl had tossed over the fence?
5. At the Sunday-school why was Tom elevated to a place with the Judge?
6. When Tom wended to school after breakfast, why was he the envy of every boy he met?
7. What did Tom begin to scrawl on the slate for Becky Thatcher?
8. When did Becky Thatcher begin to cry before Tom?
9. Whom did Tom encounter in the forest and what were the two boys dressed as?
10. Who was there with Tom when the two boys moved off wading through the tall grass of the graveyard?
11. Whose killing did the boys notice in the graveyard?
12. Into whose mouth did Tom pour down the Pain-killer?
13. What names were given to different boys when they met on the riverbank at midnight?
14. What did the people think about boys when they had disappeared?

15. What was Tom Sawyer's proudest moment of his life?
16. What was the name of the village school master and what type of book was there in his drawer?
17. How did Tom fare when he made his speech at the schoolhouse?
18. Why did Tom join the new order of Cadets of Temperance?
19. What did Tom suggest when their efforts at finding a treasure at the place of shadow had failed?
20. What did the boys went to track down?
21. Where did Huck tell Tom he would sleep while watching all night?
22. Who was with Tom in the cave?
23. Who was found dead in the cave?
24. How much money had Tom and Huck got from the treasure in the cave?

Long Questions

1. Explain how did Tom manage the white washing of the fence?
2. Describe the witnessing of their own funeral by boys?
3. Describe Tom and Becky's experience in the cave and town people's reaction to their disappearance.
4. Describe the murder of Doctor Robinson and its reaction on the boys?